GENTLE KEEPING

Prayers
and Services
for Remembering
Departed
Loved Ones
Throughout
the Year

Mauryeen O'Brien, O.P.

ave maria press  notre dame, indiana

→→→)))‹‹‹‹‹‹‹

This book is dedicated to
all those who have struggled to live
a new day
after the death of their loved ones.
May they find strength and peace
because of the struggle,
and may their loved ones live a
new life in eternal peace.

→→→)))‹‹‹‹‹‹‹

Founded in 1865, Ave Maria Press is a ministry of the Indiana Province of Holy Cross.

www.avemariapress.com

ISBN-10 1-59471-130-5 ISBN-13 978-1-59471-130-5

Cover and text design by John Carson.

Printed and bound in the United States of America.

A Prayer
of Commendation

Into your gentle keeping, O Lord,
we commend our loved ones who have died.
Though our hearts are troubled by their passing,
we hope in your kindness and tender care.
The angels have led them into paradise
where the saints welcomed them home
and every tear has been wiped away.
There we shall join them in songs of praise forever.

Amen.

—Adapted from *The Order of Christian Funerals*, #404

CONTENTS

-»»»»·«««-

INTRODUCTION

⭜⭜⭜⭜⭜⭜·⭜⭜⭜⭜⭜⭜

When we lose a loved one in death, we find that life takes on a whole new meaning. To some of us life no longer *has* meaning. To others, many of the things that once seemed so important are no longer of any interest. Our world is shattered, and we don't even have the will or the strength to pick up the pieces. One of the greatest joys in life is sharing everyday happenings with those we love. Now one of those persons is gone from us, and we wonder if we will ever want to share again. We question, "Will there ever again be anything in our life worth sharing?"

This book can help.

There is nothing unnatural or unhealthy about the way you are feeling. You are going through the grieving process because of the death of your loved one. It's a process that is absolutely necessary if you are to heal from this loss. So no matter how difficult the struggle is and how much pain is experienced, unless you work at it and persist in your efforts to move through your grief, you will not be able to rebuild your future with new meaning and purpose.

No one can take away from you the struggle that you will encounter as you grieve. The task before you is not an easy one. There is no "proper" way to do it; no certain amount of time to accomplish it; no one who can do the grieving for you. But there are things you can do to help yourself grieve well.

1

There's a wonderful little story told about a young man who was out walking one day. He happened to look down and see a butterfly shuddering on the sidewalk, locked in a seemingly hopeless struggle to free itself from its now useless cocoon. Feeling pity, he took a pocketknife, carefully cut away the cocoon, and set the butterfly free. To his dismay, it lay on the sidewalk, convulsed weakly for a while, and died. A biologist later told him, "That was the worst thing you could have done! A butterfly needs that struggle to develop the muscles to fly. By robbing him of the struggle, you made him too weak to live."

You, too, cannot be robbed of the struggle of working through your grief, for it is in the struggling that healing can begin to take place.

There are a number of things that can be of help as you begin to grieve the loss of your loved one: talking to family and friends, reading books about the grieving process, going to a support group where you can share your thoughts and feelings, spending time in quiet reflection, journaling the story of your loved one's life, remembering and celebrating that life in prayer and ritual. All of these can strengthen you, especially if they can be done with others who love and cherish you, who have a listening ear to grieve and a compassionate heart.

One particular way to grieve that we will explore in this book is the use of prayer and ritual to commemorate your loved ones. This certainly was one of the first ways you honored your loved one at the time of death. You gathered with family, friends, and neighbors at the wake service or vigil and shared many stories and memories. The funeral liturgy was a fitting tribute in prayer and ritual, as was the committal service at the cemetery. You welcomed the candles and incense, blessings and readings because they symbolized a love and reverence on the part of those gathered. Prayer and ritual at the time of death are an important way for all of us to begin our grieving.

But what happens now? You are no longer at a Church service and yet feel a need to continually remember your loved one in prayer. In the *Order of Christian Funerals*, prepared by a commission of Catholic bishops, we are reminded through the letter to the Corinthians (1 Cor 12:26) that "if one member suffers in the body of Christ which is the Church, all the members suffer with that member." The *Order of Christian Funerals* goes on to say, "The responsibility for the ministry of consolation rests with the believing community" (#9). As members of the body of Christ, we all are the believing community, charged with the privilege of consoling those who mourn. What better way can we do this than through prayer and ritual for the deceased within the atmosphere of a loving community?

Prayer "is the raising of the mind and heart to God" (*St. John Damascene*). We know that when we pray we ask God for what we need, and we thank God for what has been given us. We know that prayer can take place anywhere and that it can be either silent or vocal.

But what is ritual, and how does it interact with prayer, and how can it become part of struggling through the grieving process? "Rituals are repeated patters of meaningful acts" (Robert Fulghum, *From Beginning to End*). Our lives are full of them; we conceive them, are shaped by them; they give us structure, and they have the power to transform the ordinary into the holy. Our day becomes holy as we constantly ritualize our remembrances; and in our remembering, we heed the words of the Lord, "Do this in remembrance of me" (Lk 22:19b).

Ritual and prayer both embrace and give meaning to our departed loved ones. Both give us the strength and structure to continue our journey through grief. Both can be an intricate part of our daily, family life.

You may not feel comfortable preparing these prayers and rituals, which perhaps you once thought could only take place in church. Hopefully, this book will help you in your "ministry of consolation," by presenting reflections and suggestions for memorializing your loved ones in a meaningful way right within your home, surrounded by family and friends.

How to Use This Book

→→→》》》·《《《←←←

You can use the prayers at the beginning of this book privately or in a group setting. Many times we find it difficult to pray when we are grieving the loss of a loved one. Hopefully, these short prayers will be of help to you, especially on certain holidays and anniversaries. Read them slowly, perhaps aloud, and then give yourself some time to think about them in a spirit of quiet reflection. Ask God to listen to your prayer and grant you the peace that only God can give.

The prayer services in the second half of the book are written in the spirit of the *Constitution on the Sacred Liturgy* from the Second Vatican Council and John Paul II's apostolic exhortation *On the Christian Family in the Modern World*. They are short devotions or ritual prayers used to help those who grieve the death of a loved one. They give you and other surviving loved ones the chance to participate in communal remembrance services. They may be used by family or friends in the home (perhaps around the dining room table); within a parish setting for bereavement support or prayer groups; at a gathering of friends, relatives, or co-workers; as we pray at a gravesite; or wherever we wish to remember our departed loved one.

We are told that prayer can move mountains. Take the opportunity through prayer to climb the mountains of grief that are in your way. Every step you take is a step toward renewed strength. And every step you take is, as God told Moses, "on holy ground."

The playwright Oscar Wilde tells us, "Where there is sorrow there is holy ground." As you begin your climb, you will find that the mountains of your grieving aren't all just barefaced rock. You will find holy ground in patches of green grass, solid footholds, and perhaps even running streams to soothe you. But you must first commit to the struggle of the climb. Let prayer and ritual guide you as you climb your mountain of grief.

Simple Prayers for Remembering People, Times, and Occasions

When someone you love dies, you find, many times, that you are left numb, not able to think clearly, not able sometimes to formulate coherent communication with others. Many people say they can't even pray. They question that God is even present in their lives, as they feel abandoned and alone. Do you feel that way at times?

It is during these times that perhaps you can pick up a particular prayer in this book and let the words in that prayer speak to you and, in turn, to God. Pray it slowly, let the meaning behind the words wash over you and gently flow into your heart. Pray these prayers for your loved one and have confidence that God will not only listen to you, but also love you most tenderly for the effort you make.

PRAYERS IN REMEMBRANCE
OF PARTICULAR PEOPLE

--->>>>»>•«««<---

For a Father

Dear God,

No matter how old I will get, I will always miss my father. He was so many things to me: a provider, someone in whom I could confide, my strength, wise, generous, and loving. I know you understand this, because you are our Father who has always watched over his children and protected them. Well, that's what I am asking of you now.

Since my father is with you, embrace and bless him. Assure him that I remember him and pray for him each day. Remind him that I love him and am grateful to him for watching over me and loving me when he was part of our family here on earth. And grant, dear God, that we may be reunited one day in our heavenly home.

Amen.

For a Mother

Dear God,

Has there ever been a love that outshines a mother's? I know your Son was aware of this when he was on earth, especially as his mother stood at the foot of the cross. Her love was unbounded, self-sacrificing, simple, never demanding, always ready to give. And you lent me a mother just like that! For that I thank you! But with her death, I miss her so much. I know she is with you, but somehow I want her still with me.

And so I pray, dear God, that I am able to feel my mother's presence each day. As I was physically a part of her very being, let her now be a part of me spiritually. Let me never forget her and what she taught me and showed me: that true love is found in giving, completely and without reserve.

Amen.

For a Spouse

Dear God,

I come to you to pray for my wife (husband) and for me. We were married _____ (number) years and spent nearly every day together. We shared sorrows and joys, ups and downs, dreams and disappointments. We vowed to love each other until death, and now that time has come. She (he) is no longer here with me, but I don't want that to be an end to our love. I believe our love is so strong that it can transcend death. _____ (name) may be with you, but she (he) is also deep within my heart.

Please tell her (him) that. Let her (him) know that not even death can interfere with a love that was so powerful, selfless and lasting. Help me to hold tight to her (his) memory so that her (his) presence will remain with me until one day we are reunited together with you in heaven.

Amen.

For a Brother

Dear God,

My playmate, my friend, my protector, the one who always teased me, but loved me, has died. I miss him! He was fun to be with, and we shared many good times together. I want to recall these times and pass those memories on to the rest of the family. Somehow, we all feel incomplete without him. Perhaps by remembering together we can, as a family, still retain his presence.

Bless him, dear God. He was a good boy (man). Help those who mourn him find peace in the knowledge that he is with you. Give strength to the family, especially to me (and my siblings) who feel his absence so keenly. Draw us closer as a family, so that together we can grieve his death, but also honor his life.

Console our parents *(if they are still living)* in the knowledge that they gave life to _____ *(name)* and he, in return, lived that life well.

Amen.

For a Sister

Dear God,

What a gift my sister has been to me! We grew up together, laughed and cried, played and studied and explored; and always together, conscious of the fact that we were family. I know I still have that family, but a very intricate part of it is no longer there.

I need to capture _____'s *(name)* presence in a whole different way now. I know it can't be physical; but I long to have her still as a big part of me. Help me to gather all those cherishable memories I have of _____ together, so that we may never forget that she was and is still an intricate member of the _____ *(last name)* family.

Bless her, and bless all who mourn her. Increase in us a daily awareness that one day we will all be joined together with you in heaven.

Amen.

For a Child

Dear God,

Our little one is with you now. And I know that he (she) is in a safe, happy place, but I want him (her) with me. You lent _____ *(name)* to me for too short a time. There was so much more love that I wanted to share with him (her). There was so much more that he (she) had to accomplish here on earth. Why did you take him (her) so soon?

I need to have some answers, dear God. Please let me know that he (she) is resting in your arms right now. Hold him (her) there tightly. Tell him (her) for me that I still love him (her) and will do so for all eternity. Assure him (her), and in turn me, that one day we will be together again, that I will be able to hold him (her) once more in my embrace.

Above all, dear God, even though he (she) is with you, let me feel his (her) presence in my heart and thoughts. Never let that be taken away from me.

Amen.

For a Grandparent

Dear God,

How I loved my grandmother (grandfather), and I miss her (him). She (he) loved me unconditionally. I could do no wrong in Grandma's (Grandpa's) eyes. It was she (he) who gave me a wonderful sense of family history, traditions, and experiences. It was she (he) who told me about my own parents when they were young and taught me to see wisdom in those who have lived life longer than I have. Without my even realizing it, my grandma (grandpa) was a simple, practical, warm, and caring person on whom I could model my own life.

I pray now that she (he) can continue to be an inspiration to me, even though she (he) is no longer here. I ask you, dear God, to help me to remember the lessons my grandma (grandpa) taught me. Help me to be like her (him). Keep her (him) close to you, and grant that one day we may be united together in heaven with you where we will all experience your unconditional love.

Amen.

For an Aunt or Uncle

Dear God,

I want to pray for my Uncle_____ (Aunt _____) who has died. He (she) had a very special place in my heart and in my family. I spent many holidays and special times with Uncle _____ (Aunt _____) when I was growing up. He (she) added to those days by sharing himself (herself) and his (her) family with ours. I know I will miss him (her) during the year, especially when the family is gathered together.

Uncle _____ (Aunt _____) was very much a part of my mother's (father's) life and was able to tell me many stories about her (him). In a way those stories helped me to know my mother (father) better, and for that I will always be thankful to Uncle _____ (Aunt _____).

Bless and protect him (her), and give his (her) own family a sense of peace in the assurance that Uncle _____ (Aunt _____) is now at rest with you.

Amen.

For a Cousin

Dear God,

I will miss my cousin _____ *(name)* who has died. In a way, she (he) was like a sister (brother) to me. Although we didn't live in the same home, we had a strong bond between us. She (he) was close to my age; we seemed to agree on a lot and enjoy some of the same things. I guess in a way she (he) was a friend to me as well as a cousin. And I know that isn't always easy to find in someone.

Please bless her (him) now with your divine presence. Help her (his) family be at peace with the realization that she (he) is with you. Help all of us recall the fond memories we have of _____ so that we may be constantly reminded of her (his) goodness. I pray that one day we may all be united as family with you in heaven.

Amen.

For a Friend

O God,

I have known _____ *(name)* for a long time. I was privileged to call him (her) "friend." I was blessed to be able to talk about my deepest thoughts and dreams with him (her) over the years.

We shared so much: times, places, family events, other friends, sorrows and joys, tears and laughs. Above all, we understood and loved each other. Thank you for that.

I want to pray now for _____ and for me. For _____ that he (she) may find a home with you, who are the eternal friend. Me, that I may be open to offering to others what _____ taught me: that to experience true friendship one must be willing to trust and accept the other unreservedly.

Amen.

For a Teacher

Dear God,

So many people come into our lives and help make us who we are: our mother and father, siblings, and extended family, friends and acquaintances. Most of these we take for granted yet they are an intricate part of our lives for many years. Every once in a while we are influenced by those who may be there for only a year or two. Every once in a while we meet a teacher who sees something in us that needs to be tended to and nourished if we are to grow into responsible adults. _____ *(name)* was that teacher for me. And even though she (he) has died, the lessons she (he) taught me will be forever remembered.

Her (his) devotion, knowledge, and selflessness left a lasting impression on me and opened both my mind and heart to new and exciting things. I want to pray for _____ now and ask you to welcome her (him) into your loving arms. Thank her (him) for opening up a vast and beautiful world for me. Remind her (him) that the students she (he) taught are better people today for having been under her (his) guidance in the days they were in school.

Amen.

For a Classmate

Dear God,

It's hard to believe that someone I went to school with has died. _____ *(name)* was my age, and his (her) death certainly leaves me with many questions about my own life and death as well as his (hers). Have I lived my life to the best of my ability; did _____? Who have I reached out to over the years; whom did _____ touch? Am I prepared for death; was _____? What will happen as I live out the rest of my life; what would _____ have encountered if he (she) had lived longer?

I want to pray for _____ and for his (her) family, who I know miss him (her). And I want you, dear God, to ask _____ to pray for me. For some reason I have been given a longer time on earth than he (she) has. I want to use these years well and for you. Help me to do that! And grant _____ eternal peace with you in heaven.

Amen.

For Someone Who Has Completed Suicide

Dear God,

I have so many questions concerning _____'s *(name)* death. And all those questions begin with "Why?" "Why did she (he) do it?" "Why didn't she (he) seek help?" "Why didn't she (he) realize what this would do to her/his family and friends?" "Why didn't those who love her (him) see it coming?" "Why her (him) and not me?" But somehow I know that no matter how much I want the answers to these questions, I'll probably never get them.

And so I come to you, dear God, and ask you to be loving toward _____. She (he) needs your compassion and tenderness right now. Somehow I think _____ lost all hope and sought after the peace she (he) felt would be in a world that awaited her (him). She (he) is in that world now, dear God, and I plead with you to give her (him) that peace which she (he) needed so much. Surround her (him) with your understanding. Do not judge her (him) harshly. Extend your loving arms to her (him), and welcome _____ into your eternal embrace where we all hope to be reunited with her (him) once again and where there will no longer be a need to ask questions or to have them answered.

Amen.

For Someone Who Has Died in War

Dear God,

I saw a _____ *(soldier, sailor, marine, pilot)* off to fight in a war that he (she) believed would safeguard our country; but he (she) never came back. He (she) died defending justice and peace. I'm proud of him (her) for that, but I miss him (her) terribly.

I want to pray for _____ (*name*), that his (her) death is not in vain. I want to believe as fervently as he (she) did that the sacrifice he (she) made will bring about some good in this troubled world. Bless his (her) family who will always feel a void in their own hearts. Bless those whom he (she) fought for; and bless those whom he (she) fought against. Renew all their spirits, and revitalize the battlegrounds of this world so that the fruits of this earth may once again be used to bring life, not death.

Welcome _____ into your loving embrace where he (she) may feel eternally protected and loved and rest forever in peace.

Amen.

For a Child Who Has Been Miscarried, Stillborn, or Aborted

Dear God,

A child who was to be: who was to be part of our lives for many years, who was to bring hope and joy to the future, is no more That tiny speck of life and light has been extinguished long before it should have been. And I pray for all she (he) could have been, both in this world and to us who loved her (him) even before she (he) was born.

We are told that death is a part of life, that it is a natural happening. But I feel the death of a life that was to be and yet was never fulfilled is very unnatural, very unbelievable. And so I pray for that tiny creation of yours who will never live in this world. May she (he) find complete fulfillment in your world that has no bounds, no limits, no pain and suffering, but only love and joy and peace. And may we, who still live our lives here on earth, one day join our little one who now lives with you in heaven.

Amen.

PRAYERS FOR PARTICULAR
TIMES AND OCCASIONS

→→→⟩⟩⟩·⟨⟨⟨←←←

Morning Prayer

Dear God,

I wake up to face another day without my loved one. How I yearn for her (his) presence in my life. I keep asking myself if I can get through this day without her (him). And yet I've done just that for many days now. Somehow I've managed to find another way besides physically to have her (him) with me. It's not the same, certainly, but my memories of her (him) are giving me a strength I didn't realize I had. I know you are responsible for that, dear God, and I thank you. Just keep on helping me to remember. Help me to share those memories with others who loved her (him). Help me to listen to their stories about

_____ *(name)*, so that together we can keep her (him) a part of our everyday lives.

Dear God be with me as I begin this day. I commend my loved one to you. Bless _____. Bless me and all those she (he) loved.

Amen.

Prayer Before a Meal

Dear God,

As I prepare to eat my meal, I ask you to bless this food and bless me. May this meal give me strength for my body so that I may continue throughout this day. Help me to be aware that food is a gift from you and that it is meant to nourish me physically and sustain me spiritually.

Bless all those I love and who love me, especially _____ *(name),* who is no longer here to share this meal with me. May I be reunited one day with you and him (her) at your heavenly table.

Amen.

Prayer at Bedtime

Dear God,

The day is over, and I'm preparing to go to bed. So many times I dread doing this because I often don't sleep well. I'm tired, but I'm restless. Somehow, I can't turn off my thoughts, especially of _____ *(name).* It seems as though he (she) should be with me this evening after being absent the whole day. But I know he (she) can't be, and that makes me lonely.

I want to put myself into your hands as I prepare for bed. Help me to let go of the day with its heaviness and sadness. Let me focus on a happy memory of _____, a memory that will bring him (her) close to me. Let me awake tomorrow morning refreshed by a restful sleep in the knowledge that you have watched over my loved one and me throughout the night.

Amen.

In Winter

Dear God,

This winter season is a constant reminder to me of the death of my loved one. I look around me and see that the trees are bare; there are no flowers in the gardens; everything seems dull and dreary, cold and desolate. And I feel the same! The person who brought me so much beauty and light, warmth and joy, is with me no longer. I know it's not good for me to continually feel this way, and so I am asking you to remind me each day during this winter season that life still goes on, especially in nature, although it appears that everything is dead.

Remind me also, gentle God, that life can continue in me even though my loved one is not beside me. Help me to understand that just as the winter snows will enrich and give nourishment to the trees and flowers that now lie dormant, so, too, my memories of _____ can nourish me and give meaning to my life. Let me make the most of this winter season as a time to gather those memories and then share them with others who loved him (her) also.

Bless my loved one, and keep him (her) close to you.

Amen.

In Spring

Dear God,

Finally, spring is here! How I've yearned to see trees begin to bloom and flowers start to blossom! It's been a long, hard winter—cold and dreary. And my life has been just like that since my loved one died. I need a "spring." I long for brightness and the promise of new life. I pray for that now.

May my days be touched by the coming of spring. May my thoughts and emotions be lifted with the realization that my loved one's death is not the end, that from her (his) death an eternal rebirth is taking place with you.

Amen.

In Summer

Dear God,

Spring has turned into summer, and the earth is filled with the richness of your beauty. Gardens have bloomed, days are longer, and the workweek seems to have slowed down a bit as people anticipate and take time for vacation. I can't help but think that my vacation will be different this year because I can no longer share it with my loved one. Since _____ (name) died, I'm not even eager to take time off. It seems if I keep busy then I won't have to think about his (her) death.

Help me to realize that remembering _____ is a way that I can begin to heal. Let me use these slower–paced days, these "vacation" days, to gather my thoughts about him (her). In a way, that will be taking him (her) on vacation with me. Let these thoughts and memories strengthen me to face all the seasons of my life.

Amen.

In Fall

Dear God,

The summer with its long days filled with sunlight is coming to a close, and fall is upon us. The leaves are beginning to turn colors, and although they are beautiful in hues of red and gold, yellow, and brown, I know they will only stay that way for a while. Soon they will fall to the ground and die. I am reminded once again that my loved one, who at one time was so vibrant and alive, has now, as the changing leaves, fallen from this life and died.

I'm sad; you know that! Fall will soon turn into winter, and the harsh winds and snow will strip the trees and the landscape bare and be a constant reminder to me that I have been stripped of the presence of my loved one.

As I begin to experience the changes of this season, I ask you to remind me constantly that you will be with me as I go through the bleakness that is ahead of me. Remind me that although nature seems to be dying now, it will come alive again next spring. Teach me that death gives way to life. You showed that to me in your death and resurrection; let me be aware of that now and in the days to come.

Bless my loved one who now lives with you in eternal springtime.

Amen.

Thanksgiving

Dear God,

It's Thanksgiving, and I'm wondering what I can be thankful for now that my loved one has died. I'm not thankful for that; I wanted to spend many more years with her (him). And yet I know she (he) would want me to look beyond her (his) death and be thankful for both the time and the love we shared. I am grateful for that, dear God. Her (his) love for me was indeed one of the greatest gifts I have ever received, and the strength of it will last forever. And so, I guess I do have something for which to be thankful.

Help me, dear God, to constantly remember that gift of love; to thank you for it; and to make it so much a part of me that I can eventually share it with others. Bless my loved one and thank her (him) for being such a loving part of my life.

Amen.

Christmas

Dear God,

There isn't a place I go or a store I enter where I'm not bombarded with Christmas songs and lights and decorations and greetings of "Merry Christmas" or "Happy Holidays." I keep wondering why everything is so bright and cheery and why people around me seem so "merry." Don't they realize how painful life can be? I've lost my loved one, and it's hard for me to even think about Christmas. Christmas is a time when we should be surrounded by those we love and who love us. I don't have that this Christmas because _____ *(name)* has died.

I'm here to ask you to help me, dear God. I want to be aware, even though I'm sad, that new life was born on this day two thousand years ago. I want to believe that my loved one is experiencing that new life now. I think if I could be sure of that, I might be able to remember a little bit of the joy that surrounds this day.

Help me to believe, dear God, that my loved one is now living this Christmas with you. That is one of the best Christmas gifts I could receive this year.

Amen.

Easter

Dear God,

Easter is here! A time of remembering that suffering and death can be truly conquered; that sadness and doubt can be changed into faith-filled joy. Truly, it is a time of "Alleluia!" for your Son has shown us that life continues even beyond death.

And that is exactly what I pray for today: that the love _____ *(name)* had for me will continue beyond his (her) death, that somehow I will be able to sense, just as your apostles finally did, that love and caring did not end with death. That truly there is no end to a life that has been filled with love.

I need to believe that, dear God. I don't want to be a "doubting Thomas." I know _____ will not be physically present to me again. But let me sense his (her) presence within me. Let the love that we shared be continually resurrected in me and in all who loved him (her).

Amen.

On the Anniversary of a Birthday

Dear God,

Today is _____'s *(name)* birthday. I am so grateful that I was able to share many of those birthdays with her (him). Her (his) birth was certainly a cause for celebration, and I am happy that I was a part of her (his) life.

Today, _____ shares her (his) birthday with you. And although I know that in _____'s death she (he) is reborn, I miss her (his) presence here on earth. Help me to be thankful for the time I had with _____. Keep her (him) close to me in spirit, so that one day we may celebrate eternal birthdays together with you in heaven.

Amen.

On the Anniversary of the Day of Death

Dear God,

Today is the _____ *(number)* anniversary of _____'s *(name)* death. It's been a day I haven't looked forward to because it brings back so many difficult memories. I am filled with thoughts of the time and place of his (her) death, the cause of that death, and the unbelievable sorrow that came from it.

I need to be more positive about this date, dear God. I need to be more thankful for the many days and years I had with _____. Help me to do that. Give me the strength to begin to reflect on the cherishable memories I have of _____. Those are the memories I want to share and pass on to others who loved him (her). Help me to listen to their stories, too, so that together we can celebrate the person who _____ was and the person he (she) will continue to be in our hearts and in your eternal peace.

Amen.

On the Anniversary of a Wedding

Dear God,

Today is the anniversary of the day _____ *(name)* and I were married. What a wonderful day that was! I remember thinking I was never happier, because finally I was to be joined for life with the one I loved above all. That day itself brings back many fond memories, as do all the wedding anniversaries that followed. And I am grateful for those many anniversaries.

But here I am now, on our wedding anniversary, and _____ is not here to share it with me. I miss her (him) so. And I wish with all my heart that we had one more anniversary to be together. I need your help, dear God, to fill my heart this day so that it doesn't remain empty. Fill it with the cherishable memories and the times and places, family and friends that _____ and I shared throughout our married life. Help me to recognize that _____ can remain alive in my thoughts and prayers and heart, even though he (she) isn't with me physically. Grant that one day the love we shared together here on earth, may be eternally fulfilled with you in heaven.

Amen.

Prayer Services for Remembering People, Times, and Occasions

⇢⟫⟩·⟨⟨⟨⟨

The format for these ritual prayer services is simple, and you should modify it in any way that will help you be more comfortable or bring more meaning to your prayer. They are designed to last perhaps thirty to forty minutes, depending on how long the shared reflections last. Materials you may wish to use are listed before each service. You may decide to use different ones or none at all. You may want to use appropriate music for reflection and, on occasion, for singing. Suggested settings for each service are also provided.

Before beginning each service, read it through completely, deciding where you need to adapt what is written here. Decide who will act as leaders for the various parts of the service: the *Introduction*, the *Reflection*, and the *Ritual Prayer*. Often it is best for an adult or older teen to lead a service; at other times, anyone present might easily fill this role. Suggestions are provided at the beginning of each service.

You will also want to make copies of the reflection questions and blessing prayer for each person in the group.

Each service contains the same basic elements or parts, as described on the next page.

Introduction

This sets the tone for the ritual prayer service. One person should read this to the group, pausing after the reading for a few minutes so that the participants have an opportunity to slow down and concentrate on the reflection that will follow.

Reflection

Another designated leader reads this to the group. A series of questions are posed so that the participants may have the opportunity to silently gather some of the cherishable memories they have of their departed ones.

Silent Reflection

Quiet, reflective time is given to try to create an atmosphere of peace while each one gathers memories of their loved one.

Shared Reflection

The leader directs those present to begin to share their responses to the questions that have been asked. The leader might remind the group that they should express their honest thoughts and feelings, that there are no right or wrong answers, and that all should listen with attention and respect for one another. Each one should be encouraged to join in the sharing and be given ample time to do so.

Ritual Prayer

Read by a designated leader, the ritual prayer service should be done slowly, concentrating on the symbols presented. The entire group participates in this.

Blessing

All are encouraged to join in the blessing together.

SERVICES FOR REMEMBERING PEOPLE

Remembering a Spouse:
My Love Is Everlasting

Theme:

Love can transcend even death.

Materials Needed:

- Recording of quiet, instrumental music
- Recording of "I Have Loved You" (Michael Joncas, Glory and Praise, N.A.L.R., Phoenix, AZ)
- A ring *(perhaps a wedding ring)*
- Wedding picture *(to remain visible throughout the service)*
- Leader for service *(any family member, perhaps the spouse)*
- Reflection facilitator *(any family member)*
- Copies of the reflection questions and blessing prayer for each person

Suggested Setting:

Any place you find suitable
Living room or family room
Dining room table

Introduction

Leader:

We are gathered here today to pay special tribute and to remember _____ *(name)*, who was the beloved spouse of _____. They pledged themselves to each other in a ceremony of love years ago. We acknowledge that love and the fact that although _____ has died, the love that these two people manifested on their wedding day is a love that lives forever.

Reflection

Facilitator: *(Pause between each question.)*
- Those gathered here, spouse, family, and friends, were attracted to _____ *(name)* for many different reasons. Share what it was that you saw in her (him) that was so lovable.
- Those of us who knew_____ over the years perhaps knew her (him) as a parent or grandparent as well as a spouse. How did _____ show her (his) uniqueness in one of those roles?
- Spouses complement each other in many ways. How did you see this in the relationship between _____ and _____?
- _____ and _____ pledged their love and faithfulness "till death do us part." How do you see that love transcending death?

Silent Reflection (10 minutes)

Leader:
Take a few minutes to reflect on these questions. *(Play quiet instrumental music or "I Have Loved You.")*

Shared Reflection and Ritual

Facilitator:
We keep love alive, even after death, by sharing stories of our loved one. Let each of us do that now, using the questions from our silent reflection as a starting point. When each of us has shared our story, we will pass the ring on to the next storyteller. The ring's circular shape has no beginning and no end. Let it remind us that love is the same. It has no beginning and no end. True love continues forever.

Each one will have the chance to share their memories of _____ based on the reflection questions. As you tell your story, hold the ring in your hand. When you are finished, pass the ring to the next storyteller.

(Facilitator moderates the sharing so that each one is given opportunity to speak.)

The Church has sanctified marriage by raising it to the dignity of a sacrament. The man and woman who marry each other pledge faithfulness "for richer or poorer, in good times and in bad; in sickness and in health," forever and ever. Christ gave up his life because of his everlasting love for us. He promised, "Those who love me will keep my word, and my Father will love them, and we will come to them and make our home with them" (Jn 14:23). This becomes a model for married love. Love can be forever and can transcend death, even as Christ's love did.

Blessing (All pray together)

Lord, you showed us what true love is by your death and resurrection. Help us to keep alive the love that _____ and _____ shared together. Teach us that although our loved one's physical presence is no longer with us, her (his) memory lies deep within our hearts and can remain there forever.

Amen.

Remembering a Friend:
Through Thick and Thin

Theme:

True friendship can last forever.

Materials Needed:

- Recording of quiet, instrumental music
- Paper, colored pencils, crayons, or markers
- Copies of the reflection questions and blessing prayer for each person

Suggested Setting:

Any place you find suitable
Kitchen or dining room table
Living or family room

Introduction

Leader:

We are gathered here to remember in a special way our friend _____ *(name)* who has died. Although he (she) was not a blood relative, _____ was like a family member to us. Some of us knew _____ for a long time; some, just a short while. But no matter what was the length of time, _____ was there for us through thick or thin.

Reflection

Facilitator: *(Pause between each question.)*
- Think back to when you first met _____. What was it that attracted you to him (her)?

- A friend is one who can share our trying times as well as our good ones. What was one trying time you were able to share with _____? How was he (she) able to help you through it?
- We find many times that we are so at ease with our friend that we can laugh together. What was one incident that occurred in your lives as friends that made you laugh?
- We learn over the years to admire a person we have chosen to be our friend. What was one trait in _____ that you wish you also had? Why?

Silent Reflection (10 minutes)

Leader:
Take a few minutes to reflect on these questions (while we listen to some quiet music).

Shared Reflection and Ritual

Facilitator:
Many times when we lose someone in death, we wish we had spent more time, done more things, said what was deep in our hearts, or expressed our love and admiration for that person better. It is important that we take an opportunity to do this even though our friend is no longer with us. When you are ready, take time to share your feelings about your friendship with _____.

Ritual Prayer (After all have had time to share memories)

Leader:
When everyone has had an opportunity to share their stories, each one is invited to take paper and colored pencils (crayons or markers) and create a greeting card depicting one of those stories. As you do this, keep in mind that this is a chance to say some of the things to your friend that you didn't say before he (she) died.

(When everyone is finished, pass the cards around for all to share. This is a way you can keep the memory of your loved one alive in your hearts).

Blessing (All pray together)

Lord, you showed us by your life here on earth that you valued good friends: Mary, Lazarus, the apostles, Martha and Mary, the Samaritan woman, Mary Magdalene—to name a few. You shared your joys and sorrows, hopes and dreams, and your very self with them. Thank you for allowing our friendship with _____ to take place. May he (she) continue to enrich and bless our lives from his (her) place with you in heaven.

Amen.

Remembering a Teacher:
We Remember the Difference You Made

Theme:

Valuing the difference a good teacher can make in our lives.

Materials Needed:

- Recording of instrumental music
- Favorite books: poetry, drama, novels, short stories, etc., that each participant has been asked to bring *(see Ritual Prayer below)*
- Copies of the reflection questions and blessing prayer for each person

Suggested Setting:

Around a table (living room, dining room, kitchen)

Introduction

Leader:

We are gathered together to remember and pay tribute to our teacher, _____ *(name),* who has died. We recognize that a good teacher can make a difference in the lives of her (his) students. _____ was a good teacher, and we are better people for having been taught by her (him). We celebrate the life of _____ and the impact she (he) had on our lives in this service of ritual and prayer.

Reflection

Facilitator: *(Pause between each question.)*

- Remember back to your days in _____'s classroom. What was it about her (him) that made learning enjoyable for you?

- How did _____ make a difference in your life morally or spiritually?
- Christa McAuliffe, the schoolteacher who perished in the Challenger space shuttle disaster, once said that as a schoolteacher she "touched the future." How did _____ help mold your life intellectually so that you could "touch the future"?
- Share a story about a funny incident that happened in _____'s classroom.

Silent Reflection (10 minutes)

Leader:
Take a few minutes to reflect on these questions (while we listen to some quiet music).

Shared Reflection and Ritual

Facilitator:
When you are ready, take turns sharing your thoughts, engendered by your responses to the questions.

(Facilitator moderates the sharing so that each one has a chance to speak.)

Ritual Prayer (After all have had time to share memories)

Leader:
Many times we think we cannot adequately express the feelings we have about someone. We know we love them and that they have had an impact on our lives, but we think, "I don't have the right words." Because of that, sometimes we never tell that person how we truly feel. Perhaps that has been the case in regard to _____. Did we ever tell her (him) the difference she (he) made in our lives?

Let us do that now. We have all brought with us a favorite book. Somewhere in that book should be a line or sentence or paragraph that would mean something to us because it describes in beautiful language our thoughts about _____. Find that excerpt and share it with those here in the spirit of Jesus, the teacher, who used stories over and over in his ministry to teach about love.

(After each one is given the opportunity to read from the excerpt they have chosen.)

And now let us pray the blessing prayer.

Blessing (All pray together)

Lord Jesus, we ask you to bless this wonderful teacher who has been an important part of us. Although she (he) is no longer with us, the influence she (he) had on us has made a difference in how we live our lives. She (he) not only taught us our daily school lessons, but also how to believe in ourselves, because she (he) believed in us. Bless _____ as she (he) stands beside the greatest of all teachers for all eternity.

Amen.

Remembering a Classmate
(For pre-teens or teens. An adult should moderate.)

Theme:

Though a life is short, if lived well it can be powerful.

Materials Needed:

- Recording of instrumental music, a favorite song of the deceased classmate, or a school song
- Candles for each one attending, placed on table
- Picture of deceased on a table or desk
- Leader for service *(a classmate, if appropriate)*
- Reflection facilitator *(a classmate, teacher, or principal, if appropriate)*
- Each one attending the service is asked to bring an object or picture of an object that reminds him or her of the deceased classmate
- Copies of the reflection questions and blessing prayer for each person

Suggested Setting:

Home of deceased classmate
Friend's home
Classroom
Around a table or school desk
Lights are dim

Introduction

Leader:

We've come together because we are grieving the death of someone who meant a lot to us. _____ *(name)* only lived _____ *(number)* years here on earth. We can't help but think he (she) died too young, too soon. And it's hard for us to understand the "why" of it all. We know we really won't get an answer to "Why?" but perhaps if we gather and share our memories of _____, we will be able to hold on to his (her) presence in a whole new way, even though he (she) will no longer be with us physically.

To help us pull together these memories, we reflect on the following questions:

Reflection

Facilitator: *(Pause between each question.)*

- When did you first meet _____ *(name)*? What grade was he (she) in at that time? What do you remember most about him (her) then?
- What did _____ most like to do (hobby, sports, music, read, play video games, etc.)? Was he (she) good at it? Did you take part in this with him (her)? Was there any particular incident surrounding what he (she) did that impressed you?
- What did you and _____ talk about when you got together?
- Many times we see traits in our friends and classmates that we would like to have ourselves. What was one gift that _____ had that you would like to possess yourself? Why? How did _____ use this gift?

Silent Reflection (10 minutes)

Leader:

Take a few minutes to reflect on these questions. *(Play a selection of music from the "Materials Needed" section.)*

Shared Reflection and Ritual

Facilitator:

When you are ready, share your memories of _____, using the questions as a guide.

(Facilitator moderates the sharing so that each one is given an opportunity to speak; no need to hurry.)

Ritual Prayer (After all have had time to share memories)

Leader:

A classmate has a unique place in our lives. For the most part he (she) is our same age; we spend many years together learning and living; we are on the same teams or in the same clubs; we have the same teachers and rub shoulders with the same guys and girls. There is camaraderie among classmates and, with some, true friendship. Indeed, our classmates are a special part of our lives.

We have all brought something to this gathering that reminds us of _____. It's important for us to keep his (her) memory alive even though he (she) is no longer with us physically.

Let's each now take a turn sharing why we picked the particular object we have in memory of _____. When each of us is finished sharing, place the object on the table and pick up and light a candle. Then carefully hold that candle until all have finished.

(Leader gives time for all to share and light candles.)

Leader:

Each object you have chosen has given us a fuller picture of our classmate _____. Added to that, as each object was described, a single candle was lit until the light from all our candles and all our sharing has brought brightness to this room. As we continue over the days and years to share our memories of _____, his (her) presence will enlighten our minds and hearts so that he (she) will never be forgotten. Let us pray for him (her), and for ourselves:

Blessing (All pray together)

God our Father, we ask you to bless _____, who despite his (her) age has come to eternal rest in you. Although he (she) lived only a short time on earth, he (she) lived it well. We

ask you to continually make us aware of the gift of _____
and to one day unite us to him (her) in your heavenly presence.

Amen.

Remembering a Parent

Theme:

Our first teachers.

Materials Needed:

- Recording of inspirational music
- Bible *(preferably the family bible, if it is available)*
- Individual bibles, if available
- Small pieces of paper and pens or pencils
- Leader for service *(oldest child, if appropriate)*
- Reflection facilitator *(surviving parent, relative)*
- Copies of reflection questions and blessing prayer for each person

Suggested Setting:

Any place you find suitable
Kitchen or dining room table
Living or family room

Introduction

Leader:

We gather together to pay tribute to our parents (mother/father) who were (was) our first teacher(s) in the faith. They (she/he) taught us in so many different ways: by example, reading, instructing us, helping us prepare for the sacraments, sharing their (her/his) own faith with us, praying with and for us, and guiding us through our joys and sorrows.

Our parent(s) shared their (his/her) faith with us in the hope that someday we would embrace that faith as our own and pass it on to others. We want never to forget what our parent(s) taught us, and so we take the time to recall the faith journey we made with them (her/him).

Reflection

Facilitator: *(Pause between each question.)*

- Let us remember back to the first time our parent(s) introduced the faith to us. What particular lesson was taught?
- How did your parent(s) nourish your faith by example? (Describe one instance.)
- Was there a favorite Bible story your parent(s) shared with you? If not, what about a favorite lesson from a novel or movie? Why did this particular story have great meaning for you?
- If you were to pick out a character in the Bible who most resembled your parent(s), who would it be? How is he or she like your parent(s)?

Silent Reflection (10 minutes)

Leader:
Take a few minutes to reflect on these questions (while we listen to some quiet music).

Shared Reflection and Ritual

Facilitator:
When you are ready, take time sharing your memories of how your parent(s) passed on the Faith to you using the questions as a guide.

(Facilitator moderates the sharing so that each one has a chance to speak.)

Ritual Prayer (After all have had time to share memories)

Leader:
One of the greatest gifts parents can give to their children is to love them unconditionally. It seems that love is what opens our eyes to see the faith lived daily in people's lives. Let us open the

bible to the First Letter to the Corinthians (1 Cor 13:4–8a) and read what St. Paul tells us about love.

(If possible, all read the passage together aloud. If not, a single reader does so.)

St. Paul says in order to have faith one must first have love. He says that love is patient, kind, not envious or boastful or arrogant or rude. It does not insist on its own way, nor is it irritable or resentful. Love rejoices in truth, bears all, believes all, hopes all, and endures all things. And finally Paul tells us that love never ends.

Our parent(s), who were (was) the first to teach us the faith, did so out of love. Today, we would like to thank them (her/him) for that. Let us pick out one trait that St. Paul attributes to love that we think most exemplifies our parent(s). Write that trait on a piece of paper. As we pray our blessing prayer we will mention that trait. When we finish this ritual prayer service, we can each carry that paper with us as a reminder of the great blessing we received from our parent(s) as they (she/he) passed on the faith to us in love.

(Leader gives time for each participant to write the particular trait they saw in their parent[s]).

Blessing (All pray together)

Lord, we ask you to bless our parent(s). Thank them (her/him) for us, for showing us that faith can be lived daily through love. Tell them (her/him) how grateful we are, especially for the gift of _____ *(each person names the trait he or she wrote down).* Help us, their (her/his) children (grandchildren), to share with others the gifts that were so generously given to us. And may we one day, in faith and love, experience eternal life with you and them (her/him).

Amen.

Remembering a Child

Theme:

You will always be a part of us.

Materials Needed:

- Recording of soothing, instrumental music and/or child's music
- Teddy bear, doll, favorite game, toy, blanket, pacifier *(any one of these)*
- Picture of the child being remembered
- Leader for service *(mother, aunt, or godparent)*
- Reflection facilitator *(father, uncle, or godparent)*

Suggested Setting:

A comfortable, cozy place in the home
Picture and object chosen above, on a table so all can see
Chairs around the table

Introduction

Leader:

We have come together today to remember our little _____
(name) in a very special way. None of us can believe that she (he) is no longer here with us. All of us want to believe that she (he) is now with God in a very safe and happy place. But we miss her (him) so! And it's because we do miss _____ that we want to find a way to keep her (him) close to our hearts and a part of this family always. We can do that together by recalling the special treasure of this little girl (boy). We can do that by remembering.

Reflection

Facilitator: *(Pause between each question)*
- Why was _____ *(name)* so special to you? What was it about her (him) that was so precious?
- What did you see in _____ that reminded you of her (his) mother and/or father?
- Each child has a unique place in a family. What did you see as _____'s special impact on her (his) family?
- If you were to describe _____ to a stranger, what would you say about her (him)?

Silent Reflection (10 minutes)

Leader:
Take a few minutes to reflect on these questions (while we listen to some music).

Shared Reflection and Ritual

Facilitator:
When you are ready, take time sharing your memories of _____, using the questions as a guide.

(Facilitator moderates the sharing so that each one is given opportunity to speak.)

Ritual Prayer (After all have had time to share.)

Leader:
Jesus said, "Let the little children come to me, and do not stop them; for it is to such as these that the kingdom of God belongs" (Lk 18:16). That should give us much hope and joy for our little one. Christ assured his disciples and he assures us that children are very special to him—so special that he lets us know that not only is God's home a place *for* them but that it *belongs* to them.

Our home belonged to _____ also. And although she (he) is no longer present in it physically, she (he) can remain in it spiritually. _____ is and can continue to be a part of us always. We just need to hold on to our memories of her (him).

On the table, next to her (his) picture, is something that meant very much to _____. It was her (his) favorite _____ *(name the object)*. As we start to gather our memories, let us each take our turn holding that _____ while we share our particular story about _____. When we finish, we will pass that _____ on to the next person until all have finished.

(Take time for each person to hold the object while sharing her (his) story.)

(When all have finished)

Our stories of little _____ have all been incorporated into her (his) family story. She (he) will always be a part of the family as long as we remember and share those memories. _____'s *(name)* favorite _____ *(object)* which we place beside her (his) picture, will remain a visible symbol of her (his) place among us.

And now, let us, as family, pray a blessing.

Blessing (All pray together)

Lord God, you who blessed the little children while you were on earth, please bless little _____ now that she (he) is with you in heaven. Help us to keep her (his) presence alive in our family. Let us be aware that we can do that by continually sharing together the story of her (his) life, even though that life was too short. We want her (him) to always be a part of us as we await the time that we will be all joined together with you, as Father, Son, and Holy Spirit.

Amen.

Remembering a Sister

Theme:

A sister has many roles.

Materials Needed:

- Recording of soft instrumental music
- Something that belonged to your sister that each one present has kept as a memento *(jewelry, piece of clothing, hobby, etc.)*
- Picture of your sister, placed on a table
- Leader for service *(brother or sister if suitable, or close relative*
- Reflection facilitator *(parent if possible or relative)*
- Copies of reflection questions and blessing prayer

Suggested Setting:

Living or family room
Table for holding picture and mementos

Introduction

Leader:
One of our family members is missing from this gathering. _____ *(name)* has died, and we come together to both honor and remember her. She was a sister to me (us) through blood. She was a sister to many through her loving relationships with her family and friends. _____ came into our lives in many different ways, and we want the role she played in our lives to remain forever. In order to do that, we will try to gather our fondest memories of her and how she related to each of us in a particular way.

Reflection

Facilitator: *(Pause between each question.)*
- Let us think back to when we first became aware of _____ in our lives. What is the first memory you have of her?
- What role did _____ have in your life (sister, daughter, niece, friend, etc.)? What special way in which she lived out that role made an impression on you? Why?
- What was it about _____ that you would like to imitate in your own life? Why?
- If you had an opportunity to spend one more day with _____, what would you say to her? Why?

Silent Reflection (10 minutes)

Leader:
Take a few minutes to reflect on these questions (while we listen to some quiet, instrumental music).

Shared Reflection and Ritual

Facilitator:
When you are ready, take time sharing your memories of _____.

(Facilitator moderates the sharing so that each one is given an opportunity to speak.)

Ritual Prayer (After all have had time to share memories)

Leader:
Many times when we lose someone very close to us we tend to see him or her only in his or her principal role. She or he was my mother, father, sister, brother, etc. As we have reflected today, the same person can take on different roles as they relate to different people.

On the table we have a variety of mementos from _____'s life. Each one here has chosen something that has a special meaning to him or her.

Let us each take a turn picking up our memento for all to see. We will each hold the memento we brought as we share why it had a particular meaning in both _____'s life and in ours.

(Each person is given an opportunity to share. After each sharing, the object is replaced on the table).

(After the sharing is completed)

The table contains both a photograph of _____ and the mementos we have chosen to portray the many roles she played in our lives. Above all, we realize from all that has been spoken that she was someone who shared her love with us, no matter what our relationship with her. Let us, in prayer and blessing, show our love for her.

Blessing (All pray together)

Lord, we ask you to take _____ into your embrace. She was a blessing to us on earth as she lived out her roles of sister, daughter, and friend to us. Bless her with your love. Thank her for us for the love she gave us. Remind her that one day we will all be reunited in your eternal home, where we will live as one, heavenly family.

Amen.

Remembering a Brother

Theme:

A brother is unique.

Materials Needed:

- Recording of soft instrumental music or song from the deceased's high school or college days.
- Mementos of the person who has died *(each person should bring one)*
- Leader for service *(preferably a sister or brother)*
- Reflection facilitator *(parent or godparent, if appropriate)*
- Copies of reflection questions and blessing prayer for each person

Suggested Setting:

Kitchen or dining room table
Living or family room
Mementos on a table for all to see

Introduction

Leader:

We gather together to remember _____ *(name)* as a brother, although he was also a (son, nephew, etc.) and friend to some of us here. We wish to pray for _____, and we also want to share what each of us thought was his uniqueness—what made him so very special. Many times brothers are thought to be selfish or teasers; good in sports, but not so good in studies; hoggers of the bathroom and large in appetite; not so neat, and quite carefree in spirit. _____ may have been all, some, or none of that. It makes no difference, because he was our brother either by blood or by friendship, and as a brother he was a wonderful person, loyal and true, caring and compassionate. That's what we would like to look at and remember today: his personal gifts, his contribution to the family and the world in general, and the qualities he possessed that made him so special to us.

Let us reflect.

Reflection

Facilitator: *(Pause between each question.)*
- Let us remember back to when _____ was a little boy. What particular trait of his stood out to you? Why?
- Do you remember a funny incident in _____'s life in which he showed he had a sense of humor? What was it?
- _____ was a good brother to his siblings and son to his parents. What was one "brotherly" quality that he possessed? Name a time when you saw him use that quality in a good way.
- If you had the opportunity to speak with _____ today, what is one thing you would say to him? Is there some other way you could talk to him now besides in a physical way? How?

Silent Reflection (10 minutes)

Leader:

Take a few minutes to reflect on these questions (while we listen to some music).

Shared Reflection and Ritual

Facilitator:

When you are ready, share your memories of _____, using the questions as a guide. As you share, please hold the memento of _____ that you brought today.

(Facilitator moderates the sharing so that each one is given an opportunity to speak.)

Ritual Prayer (After all have had time to share memories)

Leader:

When we share our memories of those we love who have gone before us, we call them to be present to us, not in a physical way, but in a spiritual way. _____ was truly here with us during this time, and we have made that happen. As long as we have him within our memories and hearts, he will remain with us.

Each of us has picked out a certain object that reminds us of _____. Let's take time now to tell each other why we picked that particular object and what special significance it has for us.

(Take the time for each to pass around the particular object and share their reason for picking it.)

(When all have finished)

And now, as we each hold our memento that we will take home with us as a constant reminder of _____, let us pray.

Blessing (All pray together)

Lord Jesus, we ask you to bless _____. Though we wish he were with us physically here on earth, we are aware that he is still with us in a special way, even though he is now with you in heaven. Keep us ever aware of both your presence and his. Grant that one day we may all enjoy together your eternal presence with the Father and the Holy Spirit.

Amen.

Remembering a Grandparent

Theme:

Grandparents are special people.

Materials Needed:

- Recording of soothing instrumental music or deceased loved one's favorite music
- Something significant that belonged to deceased grandparent (e.g., sweater, prayer book, coffee cup, etc.)
- Candle
- Table on which objects and the candle are placed
- Leader for service (oldest grandchild or parent)
- Reflection facilitator (adult relative)

Suggested Setting:

Living or family room

Introduction

Leader:

We are gathered together to remember and honor our grandparents, especially _____ *(name),* who has died. We light this candle *(pause and light candle)* as a memorial to him (her). As he (she) was a light to us when on earth, so, too, he (she) will always remain a light in our eyes from his (her) place in heaven.

Grandparents are special; we know that because we have experienced their unique place in our lives. Grandpa (Grandma) played with us when we were children; was an ear to confide in as we got older; and somehow never thought we did anything wrong. It seemed that his (her) arms were always open to us, as was his (her) mind and heart. We never want to forget our grandfather's (grandmother's) love for us. So let us take some time to remember.

Reflection

Facilitator: *(Pause between each question)*
- When do you first remember Grandpa's (Grandma's) special love for you? How did he (she) show it?
- Many times grandparents take us to special places, especially when we are young. Is there one place you visited with your grandfather (grandmother) that you fondly remember? Why was that time so special to you?
- We often hear that we get wiser with age. What is one wise thing that your grandpa (grandma) shared with you? How did it help you?
- Think about a funny incident in your grandpa's (grandma's) life. What made it so funny to you?

Silent Reflection (10 minutes)

Leader:
Take a few minutes to reflect on these questions (while we listen to some music [that Grandpa (Grandma) loved]).

Shared Reflection and Ritual

Facilitator:
When you are ready, take time sharing your memories of _____, using the questions as a guide.
(Facilitator moderates the sharing so that each one is given an opportunity to speak.)

Ritual Prayer (After all have had time to share memories)

Leader:
We are all aware that each person is unique and special. Loving parents tell us that when we are young; good teachers reinforce that throughout our growing years; steadfast friends mirror it in their loyalty to us. Grandpa (Grandpa) _____ seemed to know it from our very beginning. No one seemed to be able to

deter him (her) from thinking that no matter how we acted, we were always special.

On the table are some special objects that symbolize for us something in the life of our grandparent who has died. Let us each take turns holding one of those objects that are significant to us and share with those gathered here why it means so much. When you are finished, replace the object on the table.

(Everyone is given the time to do this.)

We have each shared a unique or special story about our grandfather (grandmother). Let us now ask a special blessing on him (her).

Blessing (All pray together)

Lord God You have called a very special person, our grandfather (grandmother), home to you. We ask you to continue to bless him (her). Thank him (her) for being so caring when he (she) was with us on earth. Ask him (her) to continue to love us from his (her) place with you in heaven, so that one day we may be united together in your and his (her) loving embrace.

Amen.

Remembering a Relative

Theme:

Extended family can enrich our immediate family.

Materials Needed:

- Recording of quiet instrumental music
- Table with picture of the relative who has died
- Small pieces of paper and pens or pencils for each person
- Leader for service *(family member)*
- Reflection facilitator *(family member)*
- Copies of reflection questions and blessing prayer for each person

Suggested Setting:

Living room or family room
Dining or kitchen table

Introduction

Leader:

We gather together to honor and remember _____ *(name),* who was a member of our extended family. She (he) was someone who was related to us by blood, and so we can call her (him) "family." We didn't see _____ every day *(unless they lived with the family),* but we are grateful and privileged for the times she (he) spent with us. We shall miss those times, and so today we try to gather some fond memories of _____. These memories can help us keep _____ lovingly present among us even though she (he) has died and cannot be with us physically.

Reflection

Facilitator: *(Pause between each question)*

- Let us remember back to when we first met _____. What was it about her (him) that seemed very special to you?
- When did _____ usually visit your house? Recall one of those visits. What did she (he) add to the family by being there?
- What particular trait or gift did _____ have that you would like to have also? Explain.
- Who in your family was _____ closest to? Why do you think they were close?

Silent Reflection (10 minutes)

Leader:

Take a few minutes to reflect on these questions (while we listen to some instrumental music).

Shared Reflection and Ritual

Facilitator:

When you are ready, share your memories of your _____ *(aunt, uncle, cousin, etc.)*, using the reflection questions as a guide.

(Facilitator moderates the sharing so that each one is given an opportunity to speak.)

Ritual Prayer (After all have had time to share memories)

Leader:

Because of our shared memories, we all now have a fuller picture of _____. Each one of us, perhaps, saw something different in her (him). Each one of us had different experiences with her (him) that helped us get to know her (him).

Because we are biologically related to _____, we may have some physical likeness to her (him). We may also share some personality traits. Whatever the resemblance—physically, spiritually, or emotionally—there may well be something we saw in _____ that we would like to nurture in ourselves. Perhaps this trait will make us more like _____; perhaps it will make us a better person.

Think for a moment about the trait you saw in your _____ *(aunt, uncle, cousin, etc.)* that you would like to have yourself. Write that down on a piece of paper that is on the table.

(Leader gives time for all to do this.)

We are grateful to _____ for the special traits each one of us saw in her (him). Let us thank her (him) for possessing that gift.

Blessing (All pray together)

Lord Jesus, we ask you to thank _____ for the gift of _____ *(each one read separately, the gift they wrote on the paper)* that we saw in her (him). Thank her (him) for sharing that gift with us when she (he) was on earth. Continue to bless her (him) for us, and grant that one day we may be united with her (him) in your heavenly presence, where we will all be one family with you, the Father, and the Holy Spirit.

Amen.

(Leader asks each one to take home the paper he or she has written on and continue to thank God for the relative that was part of his or her extended family.)

Services for Marking
Times and Occasions

→→→»»»·«««←←

Beginning of a New Year

Theme:

Memories of our loved one can accompany us throughout a new year.

Materials Needed:

- Recording of soothing instrumental music and/or "Auld Lang Syne"
- Calendar for the new year
- Calendars for the year just past *(place both on a table, opened to the month of January)*
- Leader for service *(an adult male)*
- Reflection facilitator *(an adult female)*
- Copies of the reflection questions and blessing prayer for each person

Suggested Setting:

Comfortable room *(perhaps the living room or at the dining room table)*

Furniture situated in front of a fireplace

Table with calendars placed so everyone can see

Introduction

Leader:

We come together today on this first day of _____ *(year)*. We have on the table in front of us a new calendar to remind us that we all have the opportunity to begin anew. We also have the calendar of this past year. This calendar is filled with many memories, especially memories of our dear, departed _____ *(name)* who is no longer with us. We grieve his (her) death, and we continually pray for him (her). We are reluctant to begin a new year without him (her) and so must find a way to take his (her) memory with us as we go through these new days and months.

One of the best ways we can do this is to begin to gather our cherishable memories about _____. Let us look at last year's calendar and recall some of the incidents that _____ was involved in that meant so much to each of us as we reflect on the following:

Reflection

Facilitator: *(Pause between each question.)*
- What do you remember about _____that particularly impressed you during this past year?
- When was _____ last birthday? How did he (she) celebrate it?
- What was _____'s favorite month? Why? What, during that month this past year, was significant for _____ and for you in relation to him (her)?
- If _____ were here today, what do you think he (she) would tell you about "beginning again" or living each day of each year to its fullest? Why do you think he (she) would tell you that?

Silent Reflection (10 minutes)

Leader:
Take a few minutes to reflect on these questions (while we listen to some music).

Shared Reflection and Ritual

Facilitator:
When you are ready, take time to share your memories of _____, using the questions as a guide.

(Facilitator moderates the sharing so that each one is given an opportunity to speak.)

Ritual Prayer (After all have had time to share memories)
Leader:
One of the greatest gifts God gives us are our days here on earth.
To some God gives many; to others, a few. What really matters,
though, is how we use those days; how much we share God's love
with others in the days we have.

We all would like to have _____ with us during the days
of this new year. We have shared together, through our stories
how he (she) was with us last year. Those are precious and lasting memories for us.

We hope now to live out our new year getting closer to God,
to each other, and to _____. In order to do that, we must
carry our memories of him (her) throughout the year. We have
on the table a calendar for the new year. Let us each take a different month (*if the group is small some will have to take more
than one month; if it is large, the months can be repeated*); pick
out a particular day during that month; and on that date, pledge
to remember and pray for _____ in a special way. So that
each of us will be reminded of that, write _____'s name and
yours in the box depicting the date you have chosen.

(*Leader gives ample time for all to do this and sees to it that each
month is taken, then continues.*)

Now we will hang this calendar for the new year in a prominent place for all to see. Hopefully, when we come together at the
end of this year, we can share with each other how we remembered _____ in our own special way.

And now, let us ask God's blessing on _____ and on
us.

Blessing (All pray together)

Father, we ask you to bless us as we begin this new year. Bless
_____ as he (she) lives out this year with you. Help us to
keep his (her) memory alive within each of us throughout the
year. Grant that one day we may all be united in your heavenly

Kingdom where there will be no time, no days, no years, just eternity lived in love.

Amen.

(If those present wish, play or sing "Auld Lang Syne.")

Valentine's Day: We Celebrate Love

Theme:

Expressing our love.

Materials Needed:

- Recording of soothing instrumental music or a favorite love song
- Paper hearts for each one present
- Leader for service *(any family member)*
- Reflection facilitator *(youngest member present)*
- A vase of flowers
- Copies of the reflection questions and blessing prayer for each person

Suggested Setting:

Kitchen or dining room table
Family room/living room
Around a fireplace

Introduction

Leader:

Today is a special day set aside by most people to celebrate the great gift of love. Cards, flowers, candy, and gifts will be brought and given to those we love. We, as family and friends of _____*(name),* wish to express our love for her (him), even though she (he) is no longer with us. We can do that together in this ritual prayer service as we share our memories and stories about her (him). In our sharing we can proclaim the goodness and lovableness of _____ as we wish her (him) and each other a happy and blessed Valentine's Day.

Reflection

Facilitator: *(Pause between each question)*
- Our deceased love one had many gifts that made her (him) special. What is one gift that was unique in her (him)?
- Remember back to the days when you first met her (him). What was one incident in which she (he) showed her (his) love for you?
- Love is not confined to just one person; it is meant to be shared with many. When did you first notice our loved one's care and compassion for others?
- We learn from those who give love. What is one thing you have learned from your loved one?

Silent Reflection (10 minutes)

Leader:
Take a few minutes to reflect on these questions (while we listen to some music).

Shared Reflection and Ritual

Facilitator:
When you are ready, take time sharing your memories of your loved one, using the questions as a guide.

(Facilitator moderates the sharing so that each one is given an opportunity to speak.)

Ritual Prayer (After all have had time to share memories)

Leader:
A universal symbol of Valentine's Day is the heart. As a heart is physically central to life, so it is emotionally central to the expression of love that sustains and nourishes life. Christ in his public ministry reached out in love to many: the lame, the sick, the blind, sinners, the rejected. His heart was filled with love for those who had lost heart. "Young man, I say to you,

rise" (Lk 7:14b). "Your sins are forgiven" (Lk 7:48). "Take heart, daughter, your faith has made you well" (Mat 9:22b).

We each have a paper heart, a symbol of love. After hearing the different stories shared by the group, we'll take some time to write down on our heart the outline of two particular "stories of the heart" that are meaningful for us. At some time during this week or month, share these stories with someone, other than this group, who knew your loved one. Remember: "Love is not confined to one person; it is meant to be shared with many."

(*Take time to record the outline of your two favorite stories on your paper heart*).

Blessing (All pray together)

Lord, we ask you to bless _____. Through her (his) gift of love we have been blessed. Help us now to share the gifts of that blessing with others. May our love be all embracing, generous, compassionate and unselfish. Help us to be constantly aware of those who feel unloved. Keep our hearts open to them and to you who are love eternal. May our loved one rest in peace.

Amen.

Lent: As We Enter the Penitential Season

Theme:

Lent is a time of opening our arms in love.

Materials Needed:

- Recording of soothing instrumental music or a song suitable for Lent, e.g., "Were You There?," "Stabat Mater," "These Forty Days of Lent," etc.
- Two small sticks and short piece of string or twine *(to make a small cross)* for each one present
- Bible *(opened on table)*
- Leader for service *(adult)*
- Reflection facilitator *(adult)*
- Copies of the reflection questions and blessing prayer for each person

Suggested Setting:

Kitchen or dining room table
Table on which materials above may be placed

Introduction

Leader:

As we enter into the liturgical season of Lent, we are reminded that life is made up of both sorrows and joys. Many of us have received ashes on our foreheads as a sign that indeed, "we are dust and to dust we will return" (from the Ash Wednesday liturgy). We know that our time here on earth, no matter how happy or sad, is a preparation and a prelude to eternal happiness in heaven.

We are very aware of that, because someone we loved so dearly here on earth has died and is now enjoying God's presence in heaven. We are happy for that, but are sad that he (she) is no longer with us.

And so we gather to try and find a way to keep _____'s *(name)* presence alive in us somehow. We know he (she) can no longer be physically here, but spiritually and emotionally he (she) can still be a part of us. We just need to keep his (her) memory before us. To help us do that let us reflect on these questions:

Reflection

Facilitator: *(Pause between each question)*
- Think back to when you first knew _____. How did he (she) show his (her) joy? Give an example.
- All of us have sorrow come into our lives. What is one burden you know _____ had? How did he (she) handle it?
- Christ, on the Cross, gave us an example of suffering for others — a true sign of His great love. How did _____ show his (her) love for his (her) family/friends? Give an example.
- How do you remember _____ preparing for Easter during the Lenten season? What particular religious practice did he (she) have? Is there one you would like to continue during this Lenten season? Why this particular one?

Silent Reflection (10 minutes)

Leader:
Take a few minutes to reflect on these questions (while we listen to some quiet music).

Shared Reflection and Ritual

Facilitator:
When you are ready, take time to share your memories of _____, using the questions as a guide.

(Facilitator moderates the sharing so that each one is given an opportunity to speak.)

Ritual Prayer (After all have had time to share memories)

Leader:
Many times we think that Lent should be a time of great sadness. In our past we were taught that to "give up" things, such as candy, movies, dessert, etc., was the only way to observe Lent. The thought today is to do, prepare, and pray. Certainly the "giving up" is a sacrifice; but doing for others and enriching our spiritual life are also ways of preparing for the glorious resurrection of Christ and everything that glorious feast implies.

Our beloved _____ did things for others; we have all shared our memories of him (her) doing that. In a way, _____'s arms were stretched out to others many times just as Christ's arms were.

We would like to remember _____ in that way: giving to others. So that we may keep that memory symbolically before us, let us each take two small pieces of wood from the table, and entwine them with a piece of string. We will fashion them in the form of a cross.

(Leader gives time for each one to do this.)

Having finished that, let us turn to the person on our left and exchange crosses in remembrance of _____, who was always ready to share the burdens of others. (*Those gathered exchange crosses.*)

Keep those crosses in a prominent place in your home or room during Lent, as a reminder of _____'s love for those he (she) loved and of our willingness to give to others, especially at this time. This can well be our sacrifice during Lent.

And now let us thank God for the gift of his Son, who died and rose again for us and for _____, who shared his gift of love for us.

Blessing (All pray together)

God, our Father, we thank you for the gifts you give us. You shared with us your Son, who loved us unto death. You lent us our beloved _____, who blessed us with his (her) love while on earth. Bless _____, and bless us who await the eternal reunion in heaven with him (her) and with you, the Son, and the Holy Spirit.

Amen.

Easter: We Celebrate a New Life

Theme:

Death leads to new life.

Materials Needed:
- Recording of joyful instrumental music
- Candles for each one present *(not lit)*
- Large candle on the table *(lit)*
- Leader for service *(adult)*
- Reflection facilitator *(oldest child, if appropriate)*
- Copies of the reflection questions and blessing prayer for each person

Suggested Setting:

Living room *(chairs in circular arrangement around a small table)*

Evening *(if it can be arranged)*

Lights dim

Introduction

Leader:

We are gathered together as evening falls on this Easter day to remember _____'s *(name)* life here on earth and to celebrate her (his) new life in heaven. Easter evening is such an appropriate time to do that as we, the Church, have just re-enacted Christ's death and resurrection during the Holy Week liturgies. This is such a hopeful time for all of us because we know that by Christ's death on the cross, new life after death has been given to us.

So we join together in prayer to thank God for _____'s life here on earth and to ask God to embrace her (him) as she (he) enters her (his) eternal life in heaven. We do that in this remembrance service.

Reflection

Facilitator: *(Pause between each question.)*
- For those of us who can, remember back to when _____ was younger. What did you find special about her (him)?
- When _____ grew up (or was growing up) she (he) wanted to become *(or became)* a _____ *(profession, role, etc.)*. What kind of a _____ *(title)* was she (he) *(or what kind would she [he] have made?)*
- Somewhere along the line _____ touched your life in a special way. How did she (he) do that?
- If you could, how would you like to be like _____? Why?

Silent Reflection (10 minutes)

Leader:
Take a few minutes to reflect on these questions (while we listen to some quiet music).

Shared Reflection and Ritual

Facilitator:
When you are ready, take time to share your memories of your loved one, using the questions as a guide.

(Facilitator moderates the sharing so that each one is given an opportunity to speak.)

Ritual Prayer (After all have had time to share memories)

Leader:
When Christ was going through his passion and death, those around him who loved him dearly suffered with him and were extremely sad. They knew that they would lose his presence here on earth. They knew that he would no longer be around to help

and heal the people. They knew that they no longer would be able to walk with him.

We have experienced the same thing. We know that with _____'s death we no longer have her (his) presence with us here on earth; we no longer can walk or talk with her (him) _____. However, we do have our memories of _____, just as the disciples had their memories of Jesus. And we also have the same promise that Jesus made to his disciples when he was about to leave them: "A little while, and you will no longer see me, and again a little while, and you will see me …because I am going to the Father" (Jn 16:17b). That promise gave strength and hope to the disciples, and that promise can do the same for us.

Because memories can help us keep a spiritual presence of our loved one alive, let us share one gift that we knew _____ had with those here this evening. As you share that gift, please light your candle from the large candle on the table.

(*Take time to allow each one to verbalize a gift they saw in _____ as they light their individual candles.*)

(*When all have finished*)

Leader:
Our darkened room now glows with the memories we have of _____ here on earth. Here is new life from darkness and death!

Blessing (All pray together)

Lord, we ask you to bless _____ with your light and life. May she (he) be a beacon to us here on earth, as we live out our lives. May we join her (him) one day where there will no longer be darkness but only your eternal light.

Amen.

Mother's Day: We Remember Our Mother

Theme:

Our mother's unconditional love.

Materials Needed:

- Recording of soothing instrumental music or the deceased loved one's favorite music
- Packets of flower seeds for each one present
- Small dish of dirt for each person
- Leader for service *(any family member)*
- Reflection facilitator *(oldest member present)*
- Copies of the reflection questions and blessing prayer for each person

Suggested Setting:

Kitchen or dining room table

Family room

Outside picnic table

Any place you find suitable

Introduction

Leader:

We gather together on this lovely spring day in order to honor all mothers, but most especially, ours, on this Mother's Day. We will pray for her, pay tribute to, and spend time in remembering. Whether _____ *(name)* was a birth mother, adoptive mother, grandmother, aunt, cousin or friend to us, this is the day we call to mind the gifts she had that made her a woman who shared "unconditional love," as all mothers do. _____ is no longer with us physically, but she lives deep within our hearts and our memories. Let us keep her presence within us on this Mother's Day as we share those hearts and memories.

Reflection

Facilitator: *(Pause between each question.)*
- Let us remember back to when we were younger. What is one of the fondest memories you have of your mother? What has made that memory so special for you?
- Remember the most recent days of your mother. What is one thing she said to you that you would like to hold and cherish forever?
- Mothers are great teachers. What was the greatest lesson she taught you?
- How are you like your mother, or how would you like to be like her?

Silent Reflection (10 minutes)

Leader:
Take a few minutes to reflect on these questions. *(Play quiet music.)*

Shared Reflection and Ritual

Facilitator:
When you are ready, take time to share your memories of your mother, using the questions as a guide.
(Facilitator moderates the sharing so that each one is given an opportunity to speak.)

Ritual Prayer (After all have had time to share memories)

Leader:
One of the greatest gifts a mother possesses is that of nurturer. She not only gives birth, but also then spends many years and much love and energy helping her children grow. Mary, Christ's mother, did this in a very humble way. She questioned: "Son,

why have you done this to us?" But then she continued to be there to help him "grow in wisdom and understanding." So, too, with our mothers; perhaps questioning, but always there to pick us up when we stumbled; always there to help us grow; always there to love us unconditionally.

We have been given a packet of seeds and a small dish of dirt. Let us plant a few of those seeds in the dirt and in honor of our mother take them home after this service, nurture them, help them to grow. As they do, it will be a reminder to us of how our mothers did the same for us. We are who we are today because our mothers saw to it that we "grow in wisdom and understanding."

(*Take time to plant the seeds in the dirt, water them if necessary.*)

Blessing (All pray together)

Lord, we ask you to bless our mothers *(each one name your mother)*. Bless us, too, their sons and daughters. Help us to always remember that it is because of the unconditional love of our mothers that we are who we are today. Teach us to love as they did: with open arms, full hearts, and unselfish generosity. Help us one day to join with them to sing your praises in heaven, where we will never be parted from them or from you.

Amen.

Memorial Day: We Remember Those
Who Died for Their Country

Theme:

"No greater love is there, than to give up one's life for a friend."

Materials Needed:

- Recording of a patriotic song
- Map of the world or globe
- Plain stickers for each person
- Pens for each person
- Small flag of our country
- Unlit candles for each one present
- Matches
- Leader for service *(veteran, if present)*
- Reflection facilitator *(veteran, if present)*
- Copies of the reflection questions and blessing prayer for each person

Suggested Setting:

Outside picnic table, kitchen or dining room table
Above articles arranged on table for all to see

Introduction

Leader:
Our nation takes time out today to remember and honor those in the armed services who fought for and sacrificed their lives to defend our freedom. From the very beginnings of our country, those who have been part of the different branches of the armed services have been called upon to protect our rights and the rights of others. Tragically, many have died in the attempt

to gain freedom. And those here present are aware of particular loved ones who are counted among these fallen heroes.

These men and women need to be known, remembered, and honored, not only by their families, but also by a grateful people who can now live in the freedom that they died for. Let us take a few minutes to reflect on these questions concerning our particular loved one(s).

Reflection

Facilitator: *(Pause between each question.)*
- Think back to when you first knew your very special deceased veteran. What was he (she) like? What was your relationship to him (her)?
- What particular branch of the service did your loved one enter? How old was he (she)? Why did he (she) choose to be a soldier, sailor, marine, member of the air force, etc.?
- What countries did your loved one serve in? During which war did he (she) serve there?
- Where did your loved one die for his (her) country? What was his (her) funeral like? What do you remember most vividly from the service?

Silent Reflection (10 minutes)

Leader:
Take a few minutes to reflect on these questions. *(Play a quiet patriotic song.)*

Shared Reflection and Ritual

Facilitator:
When you are ready, take time to share your memories of your deceased veteran, using the questions as a guide.

(Facilitator moderates the sharing so that each one is given an opportunity to speak)

Ritual Prayer (After all have had time to share memories)

Leader:

Our deceased veterans have fought and given up their lives so that we and many people all over the world might enjoy freedom and peace. Their deaths have left a void in our lives, and we do not want them, or the sacrifice they made, ever to be forgotten. Some of them fought in distant lands and are buried there. Some lie now in cemeteries scattered throughout our nation. All, we pray, are resting with God.

So that we may continually remember them and where they spent their last days on earth, let us offer our ritual prayer in their honor.

Please take one of the plain stickers on the table and write the name of your beloved veteran on that sticker. When you have done this, place that sticker on the world map (globe), over the country in which he (she) fought and died. Then light one of the candles in his (her) honor.

(*When all have done this*)

The map (globe) in front of us represents where our loved ones gave up their lives so that we could live in freedom. Each candle represents a particular beloved veteran and is a reminder to us that although a life was given, the memory of him (her) will always burn brightly in our minds and hearts. They will not have died in vain as long as they are remembered in love. And now let us ask God's blessing:

Blessing (All pray together)

Father, we ask you to bless all our deceased veterans. They gave up their lives so that we could all be free. So did your Son. Instill in us that same spirit of self-sacrifice, and grant that one day we may all be reunited within your loving embrace, where you reign with the Son and the Holy Spirit.

Amen.

Father's Day: We Remember Our Father

Theme:

Our father's love, strength, and protection.

Materials Needed:

- Recording of soothing instrumental music or the deceased's favorite music.
- Paper, pencil, crayons, or pens
- Leader for service *(one of father's children)*
- Reflection facilitator *(father's sibling, friend, spouse)*
- Copies of the reflection questions and blessing prayer for each person

Suggested Setting:

Kitchen or dining room table
Family room
Workroom or office
Home of the deceased loved one
Any place you find suitable

Introduction

Leader:

We come together today to remember a man who had many talents and gifts but was, above all, a loving presence in our lives as a father. _____ *(name)* loved his children; he protected them, provided for them, and through his care and concern brought a strong spirit of love and devotion to his family. Today we would like to remember our father by sharing memories of him and by praying for him here, in his home (*or other much loved place*), a place he loved so much.

Reflection

Facilitator: *(Pause between each question.)*
- Let us look back to when we first remember our father. What memory of him stands out in our mind? Why is this an important memory?
- What is one thing your father told you that you want to hold on to forever?
- How are you like your father, or how would you like to be like him?
- Your father had many good qualities and talents. What is one that you found outstanding?

Silent Reflection (10 minutes)

Leader:
Take a few minutes to reflect on these questions (while we listen to some quiet music [dad's favorite music]).

Shared Reflection and Ritual

Facilitator:
When you are ready, take time to share your memories of your father, using the questions as a guide.

(*Facilitator moderates the sharing so that each one is given an opportunity to speak.*)

Ritual Prayer (After all have had time to share memories)

Leader:
We are present here in the home that our father shared with us. Each room holds a special memory of him. Perhaps we watched T.V. with him in the family room; shared the paper with him at the kitchen table; watched him fix or build things in the work room; joined him in writing an e-mail to a friend; traded ideas on how to use the computer, told and listened to stories together

at the dinner table. All these are part of the memories we have of our father.

Perhaps we never took the opportunity to thank him for the gift of himself that he gave us. Perhaps we didn't join him in the tasks he was involved in as much as we now wished we had. Perhaps we found it difficult at times to voice our love for him.

We have a means of doing that now. On the table there are paper, pencils, crayons and pens. Use whatever material you want, and begin to compose a letter to your dad, or make a drawing for him, expressing your gratitude and love to him for all that he was to you. This will be private; you don't have to share it with anyone; it will be between you and your father. The wording doesn't have to be perfect, nor the spelling. But what you write should be truly from a grateful heart. When you are finished, keep what you have written with you for awhile. It will be a wonderful reminder of the love you have for your dad. It will also remind you that you can keep in touch with your father through prayer and memories.

(The leader should give ample time to accomplish the above)

Blessing (All pray together)

Leader:

Christ thought so much of his heavenly Father that when he was asked by his disciples to tell them the best way to pray, he recited for them the prayer that we know as the "Our Father." Let us together pray that prayer.

(Leader leads the group in the "Our Father.")

At the conclusion: May the peace and blessing of Almighty God, Father, Son, and Holy Spirit, descend upon us and remain with us forever.

Amen.

All Souls Day: We Remember Those We Cherished

Theme:

Death and new life.

Materials Needed:

- Recording of instrumental music
- A single picture of a butterfly
- Pens/pencils, index cards *(colored, if possible)*
- Leader for service *(child over twelve or adult)*
- Reflection facilitator *(adult)*
- Copies of the reflection questions and blessing prayer for each person

Suggested Setting:

Around a table *(living room, dining room, kitchen)*

Introduction

Leader:

We come together today to honor those we have loved who have died. This is a day when many people throughout the world gather either in church or in their homes to do the same thing we are doing: pray and remember the faithful departed. Those we love may have died recently or a while ago. But no matter how long it has been we still wish to honor them in prayer as we gather as family and friends. We shall never forget them. They were an intricate part of our lives while they were with us on earth. They shall remain the same as they love and intercede for us from heaven.

Reflection

Facilitator: *(Pause between each question.)*
- Though we all know a number of people who have died, which one were you closest to? Why?
- What particular gift did that person possess that attracted you to her or him?
- Did that particular person help make you a better person? How?
- What is one story about that person that you would like to pass on to others?

Silent Reflection (10 minutes)

Leader:
Take a few minutes to reflect on these questions (while we listen to some music).

Shared Reflection and Ritual

Facilitator:
When you are ready, take time sharing your memories of your particular loved one, naming the person and her or his relationship to you, using the questions as a guide.

(*Facilitator moderates the sharing so that each one is given an opportunity to speak.*)

Ritual Prayer (After all have had time to share memories)

Leader:
Many times when we experience the death of a loved one we feel that life is over both for the person who has died and for ourselves. We grieve because that person will no longer be physically with us. We grieve because we will no longer hear her or his voice or see them grow and change and enjoy the beauty that surrounds them or know the people who love them. Sometimes

we feel that life has no more meaning because those who gave so much meaning to our lives are no longer with us.

What we sometimes fail to see in sorrow is that from death comes new life. We see this in nature each day: the seed falls to the ground in the winter, and is apparently dead, only to blossom into a living beautiful thing as spring appears. The cocoon and all that it contains seem to us to be ugly and useless, yet as the butterfly emerges and sheds its dying cocoon, a new and beautiful life is born. Christ, having died and been buried, burst forth from the tomb on Easter morning, alive and glorious, bringing new life and new hope to those who had lost all hope in life. Today we have embraced our loved one's presence in our lives by the memories we have shared together. New life has come from death for her or him. And that new life is in the Lord and in us if we keep our memories of her or him alive in our hearts and minds.

In order to help us do that, we each will take an index card and draw on it a simple picture of a butterfly, a symbol of life from death. Underneath the picture print the name of your loved one and one word that symbolizes for you a trait or gift she or he had, that you would like to have in your own life (example: peace, joy, laughter, etc.). Carry that card with you for a while as a reminder of your loved one's gift to you. Pray that this gift may become strong within you, and thank your loved one for sharing it with you.

(Take time for all present to complete the index card.)

(When all have finished)

And now let us pray the blessing prayer, remembering that from death your loved one now lives a new life in heaven and in our hearts.

Blessing (All pray together)

Lord God, we ask you to bless our loved ones, especially
_____ (*each one name the particular person they are praying*

for). From death she (he) now lives a new life with you. Help us to be aware that she (he) is still alive to us in our hearts and minds. On this Feast of All Souls, we remember all who have died and now enjoy your eternal presence. May they and we one day enjoy that life together in heaven where there will be no sorrow or loss but only life and light.

Amen.

Thanksgiving: We Give Thanks

Theme:

A toast to remembrance.

Materials Needed:

- Recording of a Thanksgiving song or hymn, or instrumental music
- A drink at the table *(wine, water, soda, milk, etc.)* to toast with
- Leader for the service *(mother, father, or grandparent)*
- Reflection facilitator *(oldest member present)*
- Copies of the reflection questions and blessing prayer for each person

Suggested Setting:

Dining room or kitchen table that is set for the Thanksgiving meal. All are seated around it before the meal is served.

Introduction

Leader:

We have come together as an extended family to celebrate and give thanks for the many blessings we have received during this past year. We pick this particular day because traditionally here in the United States, the first settlers joined with their Native American neighbors to do the same thing. This is a festive holiday during which we "count our blessings" for the simple gifts of the earth that sustain us: food, drink, shelter, and the love that family and friends extend to us.

One of our family members (friends) is no longer with us physically. We grieve that because we dearly love him (her). But we will feel his (her) presence in a different way today because we will take the time to not only remember him (her) in a special way, but to share together what we wish to thank him (her) for.

Reflection

Facilitator: *(Pause between each question.)*
- Let us remember when we first became aware of _____ *(name)* in our lives. What quality stood out about him (her)?
- How have you seen that quality grow over the years? Think of examples.
- If you had the opportunity to say thank you to _____, what particularly would you thank him (her) for?
- What trait did _____ possess that you would like to have yourself? Why?

Silent Reflection (10 minutes)

Leader:

Take a few minutes to reflect on these questions. (*Play a Thanksgiving song or soft instrumental music.*)

Shared Reflection and Ritual

Facilitator:

When you are ready, take time sharing your memories of _____, using the questions as a guide.

(*Facilitator moderates the sharing so that each one is given an opportunity to speak.*)

Ritual Prayer (Takes place immediately or after the meal is eaten and before dessert is served. All should be present at the table. Be sure all glasses have been filled.)

Leader:
We have shared some of our fondest memories of _____
today. This has helped make him (her) very present to us
here at our Thanksgiving table. This is very fitting because
_____ is still very much a part of us even though he
(she) isn't here physically.

Christ had that same thought in mind when he commissioned
the apostles to change bread and wine into his body and blood
"in remembrance of me" (Lk 22:19b). He knew he could remain
present to them and to us through the Eucharist. He knew that
presence did not always have to be physical in order to be real.
We have remembered _____ through our shared stories.
He (she) has been present to us through them and can continue
to be as we remember him (her) over the years to come.

We all have a filled glass in front of us. Let us each raise our
glasses and individually toast _____ in the form of a
Thanksgiving blessing for the particular presence he (she) had in
our lives.

Blessing (Leader goes first)

Leader:
I want to thank _____ *(name)* for the gift of
_____, to me *(name the particular trait you saw in
him [her] that touched you)* and ask our God to bless and keep
him (her) for all eternity. *(Leader raises the glass takes a sip, and
invites all to do the same.)*

*(Continue around the table, each person taking a turn. When
everyone is finished, all raise glasses once more and conclude the
blessing.)*

With heartfelt thanks, we pray.

Amen!
(Dessert is served.)

Advent: We Remember as We Prepare to Begin Advent

Theme:

Preparing for new beginnings.

Materials Needed:

- Recording of instrumental or Advent music (e.g., "O Come, O Come Emmanuel")
- Four small candles for each family represented
- A small wreath, four candleholders, or a small bowl of sand for each family represented
- Matches
- Leader for service *(any adult)*
- Reflection facilitator *(any adult)*
- Copies of the reflection questions and blessing prayer for each person

Suggested Setting:

First Sunday of Advent, if possible
Kitchen, dining room, family room, or living room
Table to place candles, wreath, holders, bowl of sand

Introduction

Leader:

As we gather on this first Sunday of Advent, we are aware that the Church celebrates the beginning of a new liturgical year and bids us to prepare spiritually for the commemoration of the birth of Christ. As the world around us becomes excited and alive with the festivities surrounding the Christmas season, we take a few quiet moments to ponder the true meaning of Christmas and how that relates to our loved one's death.

There is someone who will not be here with us physically this Christmas. That makes us sad in one sense, and yet if we truly join in the spirit of this Advent season, there is hope for us that _____'s *(name)* presence will be felt among us. Advent is all about preparing for a new beginning with the birth of Christ. _____'s life was preparation for the new beginning she (he) is now experiencing in heaven. Remembering her (his) life can help us take part in the joy of that new beginning with and for her (him).

Let us take the time together now to gather our memories of _____'s life that we feel were steps toward her (his) new life with God.

Reflection

Facilitator: *(Pause between each question)*
- When did you first become aware of _____ in your life? What was your relationship to her (him)?
- What do you remember about _____ in regard to Christmas?
- How did you see _____ face new things (e.g., new activities, new challenges, new people) in her (his) life?
- Prayer and good works are great preparations for heaven. What is memorable to you in _____'s life in regard to prayer and good works?

Silent Reflection (10 minutes)

Leader:
Take a few minutes to reflect on these questions (while we listen to some quiet music).

Shared Reflection and Ritual

Facilitator:

When you are ready, take time sharing your memories, using the questions as a guide.

(*Facilitator moderates the sharing so that each one is given a chance to speak.*)

Ritual Prayer (After all have had time to share memories)

Leader:

As the Church begins its new liturgical year and its preparation for Christmas with the beginning of Advent, we take the time today to look at new beginnings both in our own lives and in the life and death of our beloved _____. How are we preparing to celebrate the spiritual coming of Christ in our lives? How did we see _____ prepare during the past Advent seasons? What can we do to increase our spiritual preparation for a new beginning? How can we include _____ in that preparation so that on Christmas Day we become more aware of Christ's presence as well as _____ in our lives?

We have in front of us the material to put together a visible reminder of this preparation time—the ingredients for an Advent wreath or something to hold our four candles representing the four weeks preceding Christmas. Each family can light the first candle after we have situated it either in the wreath, in the holder, or in the sand. As we light it, let us take turns sharing with the group one particular gift _____ had that showed us she (he) was preparing spiritually as well as physically for the coming of Christ both at Christmas and also each day in her (his) heart.

(*Take the time for each family member to do that.*)

(*When all have finished*)

Let us say together, "Come, Lord Jesus." (*Repeat.*) We ask each family to take this Advent symbol home and repeat the same ritual at the beginning of each week with the remaining candles, saying as the candle is lit, "Come, Lord Jesus." And now let us pray the blessing prayer.

Blessing (All pray together)

Lord Jesus, we ask you as we prepare for your coming into our hearts this Christmas when to bless all whom we love, especially our newly departed _____. Grant her (him) a new beginning with you in heaven. Grant us the realization that she (he) can continually be with us in a new way because death has only brought her (him) to new life.

Amen.

Christmas

Theme:

Our loved one as part of our Christmas celebration.

Materials Needed:

- Recording of Advent music or Christmas instrumental music
- Christmas tree decorated but not lit
- Christmas ornaments *(one selected beforehand by each person present)*
- Leader for service *(family member)*
- Reflection facilitator *(parent or aunt, uncle, or grandparent)*
- Copies of the reflection questions and blessing prayer for each person

Suggested Setting:

Wherever the Christmas tree stands, with all or some of its lights turned off

Introduction

Leader:

We are gathered around our Christmas tree, which we know has been part of our celebration of Christmas for many years. We've taken the time to select just the one we want; we've strung the lights; placed the ornaments just so; covered the branches with tinsel or strings of popcorn; and topped the tree with the angel or star we have used each year. Soon we (Santa) will place the gifts under the tree. But before we open our gifts at just the right time, we will, as a family (group), celebrate together the true meaning of Christmas: Christ's presence among us.

We are all sadly aware that _____ *(name)* will not be with us this year as we celebrate. His (her) Christmas will be in heaven. That makes us both happy and sad. We are happy because _____ is now with God, yet sad because he (she) is not with us.

But we want _____ to be part of our celebration. We want to remember him (her) as we light our tree. We want to remember that he (she) was a gift to us while he (she) was with us as we open the gifts that are under the tree. We want to be aware that he (she) is still present to us in a very special way.

Reflection

Facilitator: *(Pause between each question)*

- _____ gave himself (herself) to us during his (her) lifetime in many unique ways. How did he (she) share himself (herself) with you?
- If _____ were here this evening, what particular part would he (she) take in this celebration? What would he (she) do or say?
- If you had the opportunity to give _____ a gift this Christmas, what would it be? Why would you give that particular gift?
- What has made _____ so special in your life?

Silent Reflection (10 minutes)

Leader:
Take a few minutes to reflect on these questions (while we listen to some quiet music).

Shared Reflection and Ritual

Facilitator:
When you are ready, take time sharing your memories of _____, using the questions as a guide.

Ritual Prayer (After all have had time to share memories)
Leader:
Our tree stands straight and tall, filled with lights ready to be lit; ornaments carefully selected; tinsel or popcorn adding to the fullness and beauty of it. We know that the lighting and decorating of the Christmas tree by the family is a tradition that is carried on in hundreds and hundreds of homes. Our home is different this year because one of our family members is no longer physically present with us. We have shared remembrances of him (her), and that has given us the opportunity to have _____ present in a different way; he (she) is with us here, in our hearts and in our minds, our thoughts and our emotions.

We would like to have a visible reminder of that, one that will last not only this Christmas Eve, but throughout the Christmas season and even beyond.

We have each brought a special ornament that we will place on the tree. Let that ornament be _____'s ornament. Every time we see it, it will be a reminder that _____ is a part of this celebration and that he (she) has a prominent place in our Christmas celebration and is alive in our hearts as he (she) lives out eternal life.

As you place _____'s ornament on the tree, please share what was so special about _____ to you, something that has helped make you who you are today.
(*Give each one the opportunity and the time to do this.*)

Blessing (All pray together)

As we celebrate the feast that commemorates your coming among us, dear Lord, may we be aware of your presence in our lives. May the tree and the lights and ornaments that we have placed on it be a constant reminder of your great love for us. Help us to remember _____ again and again and the gifts he (she) gave to us, especially in his (her) presence in our lives. Let us feel that presence in a special way this Christmas season.

Amen.

(*Leader lights the Christmas tree*)

Leader:

Dear Lord, may your light reflected in this tree lead us, as it has led _____ to eternal light and life.

Amen.

(*All sing "O Christmas Tree" or any other suitable Christmas hymn.*)

Anniversary of the Day of Death:
We Remember That Special Day

Theme:

Anniversaries help us remember.

Materials Needed:

- Recording of soothing instrumental music or the deceased loved one's favorite music
- Candles on a table for each one present
- Large candle on the table where a picture of the deceased is in a prominent place
- Leader for service *(anyone)*
- Reflection facilitator *(close family member)*
- Copies of the reflection questions and blessing prayer for each person

Suggested Setting:

Any place you find suitable, preferably in the evening after dark

Dining room table

Living or family room

Porch or deck

Introduction

Leader:

We are here this evening on the anniversary of the death of our loved one, _____ *(name)*. She (he) left us on this day, _____ *(number)* year(s) ago. Remembering back to that day can be very painful. Although we realize it can't be, we always want those we love to remain with us forever. We know now that _____ cannot be here physically for us again, and so we strive to find another way for her (him) to be present to us. Celebrating this anniversary can help do that, for in the remembering, _____ can remain part of us emotionally and spiritually. That presence can truly be part of us forever and brighten our lives.

The large candle on the table is a symbol of Christ. It will be lit to remind us that although it is dark all around us, the light of remembrance can pierce that darkness and begin to brighten both our days and our nights. Let us begin to add to that single light the flame of our memories of _____.

Reflection

Facilitator: *(Pauses between each question.)*
- Let us remember one particular gift that _____ shared that helped make our world a little brighter. How did that help you personally?
- What is your fondest memory of _____?
- _____'s light and life touched many people. Think of someone you know, besides yourself, who, _____ reached out to. How, particularly, did she (he) touch them?
- Many times if a light is strong enough, it reflects whatever surrounds it. How have _____'s family and friends reflected the goodness of her (him). In what ways can you see this?

Silent Reflection (10 minutes)

Leader:
Take a few minutes to reflect on these questions (while we listen to some music).

Shared Reflection and Ritual

Facilitator:

When you are ready, take time sharing your memories and thoughts of _____, using the questions as a guide.

(*Facilitator moderates the sharing so that each one is given an opportunity to speak.*)

Ritual Prayer (After all have had time to share memories)

Leader:

We have had many "lights" in our lives. Our parents were the first ones to show us the way to live our lives in light and not darkness. Our teachers spent years enlightening our minds so that we could begin to envision a future that would be bright and successful. Our family and friends encouraged us to move forward and not stumble in the darkness. We were taught to appreciate light because it was a sign of life lived openly in joy and in peace.

Throughout the New Testament, light is a symbol of Christ, who told us that he was the light of the world and that "the light shines in the darkness, and the darkness did not overcome it" (Jn 1:5). That is the divine light that we yearn to possess. That is the light that _____ now possesses.

There are a number of small candles on the table. Let us each take one and begin to light our candles from the light of the large one. As we do, the brightness in the room will expand and give life to places that we can't yet see. We will take our lights from the one large candle, the symbol of Christ among us, and infuse the entire room. Our sharing of memories has enriched the lives of those around us and kept _____ alive in our hearts and minds. That is the celebration that this anniversary brings to us. And so we light our candles.

(*Each person takes a smaller candle and lights it from the large one.*)

(When all candles are lit)
Then let us pray together:

Blessing

Lord, on this _____ *(number)* anniversary of
_____'s death, we are aware that she (he) is no lon-
ger with us physically. For so long that has caused us to live in
darkness. We don't want to continue doing that anymore. We
realize that _____ was a light to us, and we wish to
spread her (his) light to others. We know we can do that by sharing our memories of her (him). And so we ask your blessing on
_____ and on us as we go forth from this place, continually remembering that you will be our everlasting light and
that _____ lives in that light with you forever.

Amen.

Anniversary of a Birthday:
Good News of Great Joy

Theme:

We celebrate the birthday of our loved one who has died.

Materials Needed:

- Recording of soothing instrumental music or favorite music of the loved one
- Birthday cake, plates, forks, napkins, and knife
- Picture(s) of the deceased loved one to be displayed during the service
- Large candle
- Leader for service *(any family member)*
- Reflection facilitator *(any family member or close friend)*
- Copies of the reflection questions and blessing prayer for each person

Suggested Setting:

Kitchen, dining room, or picnic table
Above material placed on table

Introduction

Leader:

We gather together as family and friends to celebrate the anniversary of the birth of _____ *(name)*. Although he (she) cannot be a physical part of this celebration, he (she) will be very present to us as we share our memories. As we light this candle and place the picture(s) of our loved one before us, we are reminded that he (she) shares in the eternal life and light of God. May that light shine upon us this day as we call to mind the life of our dear one. As that life was a part of us when _____ was with us here, let our sharing together remind us that he (she) is still part of our lives.

Reflection

Facilitator: *(Pause between each question.)*
- If you were there, try to remember _____ as a baby or a young child. What was he (she) like?
- Each member of a family adds something unique to the family unit. What particular gift did _____ have that enhanced the spirit of the family?
- Birthday parties are a time of great festivity and joy. Recall one such party for _____ and describe a joyous event that occurred at it.
- One of the traditions at a birthday celebration is to give gifts. What gift from you would you want _____ to have if he (she) were physically present at this birthday celebration today?

Silent Reflection (10 minutes)

Leader:
Take a few minutes to reflect on these questions (while we listen to some quiet music).

Shared Reflection and Ritual

Facilitator:
When you are ready, take some time to share your memories, using the questions as a guide.

(*Facilitator moderates the sharing so that each one is given the opportunity to speak.*)

Ritual Prayer (After all have had time to share memories)

Leader:

Many times when we attend a celebration of some sort, we are offered food and drink as part of that celebration. We see this at various times in the life of Jesus: The Wedding at Cana (Jn 2:1–11), Feeding of the Five Thousand (Mt 14:13–21), and Institution of the Lord's Supper (Lk 22:15) are some notable examples. Jesus used food and drink as expressions of joy and festivity.

We have a cake here to celebrate the birth and life of _____. Please cut a piece of birthday cake for yourselves. When everyone has done this, let us sing that famous birthday song that has come down to us from ages past, and then together have our piece of cake in honor of _____, whose birth brought us "good news of great joy."

(*Take time to pass the cake, cut the pieces, to sing, and then to enjoy the birthday cake.*)

Blessing (All pray together)

Lord, the angels sang with great joy at your birth, "Glory to God in the highest heaven, and on earth peace among those whom he favors" (Lk 1:14). So, too, we express our joy because _____ was born. As we celebrate the anniversary of that birth, help us to feel the peace that we know you wish us to have. Help us to remember always that _____ was your gift to us and for that, though he (she) is with us no longer, we are eternally grateful.

Amen.

Anniversary of a Wedding:
We Remember a Forever Love

Theme:

True love lasts beyond death.

Materials Needed:

- Recording of soothing instrumental music
- Two plain rings *(preferably wedding rings)* on a plate, placed on table
- Two lit candles on table
- Leader for service *(adult relative or in-law of deceased spouse)*
- Reflection facilitator *(adult relative or in-law of deceased spouse)*
- Copies of the reflection questions and blessing prayer for each person

Suggested Setting:

Living or family room

Chairs surrounding a table with the above-listed objects on it

Introduction

Leader:

We gather together around this table that contains two candles, symbolizing the joining of two families at the wedding of _____ and _____, _____ *(number)* years ago. On the table are also two rings to remind us of the wedding bands worn by this husband and wife. By their very design, they represent a love that will never end. Some of us witnessed that love proclaimed on their wedding day. Others saw it lived

out in their lives each day. It would be good for us to reflect now ,
on how we saw that eternal love especially in the life of our dear,
departed _____ (*name of deceased spouse*).

Reflection

Facilitator: (*Pauses between each question*)
- When were you first aware of _____'s great capacity
  to love? How did he (she) show this?
- Love manifests itself in good works or works of service
  to others. Did you ever see this in _____? What
  example stands out to you?
- Today is the anniversary of the wedding of _____
  and _____. How did you see their love grow
  over the years since that day?
- The love between a man and woman can overcome many
  obstacles if they are determined to face their problems
  together. When were you first aware that _____
  and _____ worked as a team through difficult
  times? Give an example of that.

Silent Reflection (10 minutes)

Leader:
Take a few minutes to reflect on these questions (while we listen
to some quiet music).

Shared Reflection and Ritual

Facilitator:
When you are ready, take time sharing your memories of
_____, using the questions as a guide.

(*Facilitator moderates the sharing so that each one is given an
opportunity to speak.*)

Ritual Prayer (After all have had time to share memories)

Leader:

We are all aware of the story of the Last Supper. Christ so loved his apostles and us that he left a memory of himself in the form of bread and wine. He said that he would "not leave [us] orphaned." He said, "In a little while the world will no longer see me; because I live, you will also live" (Jn 14:18–19). All that Christ asked of the apostles, and so of us, was that we love.

Love, and therefore living in Christ, is certainly the foundation of marriage. We saw that in the marriage of _____ and _____. That love was promised "till death do us part." That love was symbolized by the wedding rings that are designed as one piece having no beginning and no end.

Let us pass around these rings that are on the table. Each one hold them for a minute, letting their unending roundness symbolize for us the love that _____ and _____ had for each other in marriage and that now reaches beyond death. Their love will never end and but reach fulfillment when one day they are united once more in the embrace of our loving God, who was an intricate part of their marriage.

(*Leader gives everyone the time and quiet to do this.*)

Blessing (All pray together)

Lord, we know that true love never ends in death. If it is strong, unselfish, and caring, it continues beyond this earthly life. Let all of us feel _____'s love from heaven, especially his (her) spouse, _____. Grant that the love they manifested so beautifully throughout their married life be a constant inspiration (to their children and) to all whom they hold dear. Grant that our love, like theirs, will always be strong enough to reach beyond death to your eternal home.

Amen

We Light a Candle for You:
A Candlelight Remembrance Service

(For any ordinary time or special occasion)

Theme:
Our deceased loved ones can be a light to us.

Material Needed:
- Recording of quiet instrumental music or the deceased loved one's favorite music
- Candles for each one present
- One large candle and a bible
- Table
- Leader for service *(anyone from group)*
- Reflection facilitator *(anyone from group)*

Suggested Setting:
Any comfortable place where a group can assemble *(preferably in the evening)*
Single candle *(lit)* and bible *(opened to Jn 8:12: "I am the light of the world.")*
Candles placed on a table
Lights dimmed, if appropriate

Introduction
Leader:
We gather together to honor our loved one, _____ *(name),* in a candlelight service of remembrance. We are all aware of the darkness we have felt because of _____'s death. We have all struggled through that darkness and now long to see the light. And so we've come to spend some time in gathering our

memories of _____ and sharing those memories with one another. So that we can do that, let us spend a few minutes recalling what _____ meant to each of us personally.

Reflection

Facilitator: *(Pause between each question)*
- How would you describe _____ to someone who had never known him (her)?
- What was it about _____ that made him (her) so very special to you? Give an example.
- Recall a funny story or time associated with _____. Why was it particularly funny to you?
- If you could spend another day with _____, what would you do and say?

Silent Reflection (10 minutes)

Leader:
Take a few minutes to reflect on these questions (while we listen to some music).

Shared Reflection and Ritual

Facilitator:
When you are ready, take time sharing your memories of _____, using the questions as a guide.

(Facilitator moderates the sharing so that each one is given an opportunity to speak.)

Ritual Prayer (After all have had time to share memories)

Leader:
By sharing our memories of_____ we have all honored him (her) in a special way. By sharing those memories we have all been enriched. This has honored _____ also. We can now show our love for him (her) in a special, visual way. Let each of us light one of the candles on the table from the large candle

that has been placed alongside the Word of God. As we light the candle, we can each mention aloud one gift that you think _____ had—a gift that he (she) shared with others or perhaps with you in particular. *(Leader gives examples of a "gift," i.e., humility, peace, laughter, wisdom, etc.)*

(After all have lit the candles and mentioned a gift the deceased loved one possessed)

You see how the gifts that _____ possessed and shared with others have given bright light to this once darkened room. Our lives have become richer and fuller because we knew and loved _____. We will always be grateful for that. We will always be grateful to _____.

And now let us ask God to bless our beloved _____.

Blessing (All pray together)

God, our Father, we ask you to love and bless _____ as he (she) lives now with you in heaven. Let us always feel his (her) presence as a light within us, leading us eventually to join him (her) in your eternal presence, where you live with the Son and Holy Spirit.

Amen.

Record of Famly Deaths
⤜⤜ We Remember ⤜⤜

Name   **Relation**

_____   _____

_____   _____

_____   _____

_____   _____

_____   _____

_____   _____

_____   _____

_____   _____

_____   _____

_____   _____

_____   _____

_____   _____

_____   _____

_____   _____

_____   _____

_____   _____

	Date of Birth	Date of Death

ACKNOWLEDGMENTS

I am grateful to all those who have allowed me to walk their journey of grief with them. They are all an intricate part of this book as together we pray for healing and peace.

Special thanks go to Cecelia O'Brien and Joseph Cadella for their assistance in the assembly of this text, to Bob Hamma of Ave Maria Press who encouraged me to write it, and Eileen Ponder for her suggestions and editing skills.

SR. MAURYEEN O'BRIEN, O.P., is coordinator for ministry to the bereaved, separated, and divorced for the Archdiocese of Hartford, Connecticut. She is past president of the Board of Trustees for the National Catholic Ministry to the Bereaved. A native of New York and graduate of the University of Notre Dame, O'Brien is also a member of the Dominican Sisters of St. Mary of the Springs.